The Jail Is Everywhere

The Jail Is Everywhere

Fighting the New Geography of Mass Incarceration

Edited by Jack Norton,
Lydia Pelot-Hobbs,
and Judah Schept

Foreword by Ruth Wilson Gilmore

VERSO

London • New York

First published by Verso 2024
Collection © Verso 2024
Contributions © Contributors 2024

1 3 5 7 9 10 8 6 4 2

Verso
UK: 6 Meard Street, London W1F 0EG
US: 388 Atlantic Avenue, Brooklyn, NY 11217
versobooks.com

Verso is the imprint of New Left Books

ISBN-13: 978-1-80429-131-3
ISBN-13: 978-1-80429-132-0 (UK EBK)
ISBN-13: 978-1-80429-133-7 (US EBK)

British Library Cataloguing in Publication Data
A catalogue record for this book is available from the British Library

Library of Congress Cataloging-in-Publication Data

Names: Norton, Jack (Editor of The jail is everywhere), editor. |
  Pelot-Hobbs, Lydia, editor. | Schept, Judah Nathan, editor.
Title: The jail is everywhere : fighting the new geography of mass
  incarceration / edited by Jack Norton, Lydia Pelot-Hobbs, and Judah
  Schept ; foreword by Ruth Wilson Gilmore.
Description: London ; New York : Verso, 2024. | Includes bibliographical
  references.
Identifiers: LCCN 2023030891 (print) | LCCN 2023030892 (ebook) | ISBN
  9781804291313 (trade paperback) | ISBN 9781804291337 (ebook)
Subjects: LCSH: Jails—United States--Design and construction.
Classification: LCC HV8827 .J355 2024 (print) | LCC HV8827 (ebook) | DDC
  365/.5—dc23/eng/20231017
LC record available at https://lccn.loc.gov/2023030891
LC ebook record available at https://lccn.loc.gov/2023030892

FSC
MIX
Paper | Supporting
responsible forestry
FSC® C171272

Typeset in Sabon by MJ & N Gavan, Truro, Cornwall
Printed by the CPI Group (UK) Ltd, Croydon CR0 4YY

Contents

Foreword

Ruth Wilson Gilmore

It's difficult to fight an adversary that keeps changing shape. The narrative momentum of horror movies depends on the terror of scary surprise to keep audiences riveted to the improbable by presenting it as inescapable—at least until some resourceful protagonists, frequently with their backs against the wall, outsmart the monster using creative aggression.

How do protagonists outsmart a monster? They figure out how it works and what it needs. The key: a combination of curiosity and persistence. Chance plays a role, but they also notice patterns—the two combined in study of the objective and subjective elements of monstrous structure and agency. In and through the process of understanding and defeating the monster, protagonists themselves change, becoming different from how they were when they started out.

By showing how fighting protagonists figure out the ideological, material, and political eruptions of the jail, this book demonstrates its monstrous strengths and vulnerabilities. These chapters vividly detail the monster's existential necessities: land, labor, money, state capacity. A jail lacking opposition nestles into landscapes and consciousnesses as an appetite that naturally, necessarily, and inevitably devours people, communities, and lives. But time and again people seize alienation as a productive force of creative aggression—whether prompted by curiosity, anger, experience, comparison, or something else—refusing to be spectators to their own systemic and individual demise.

Active awareness prompts multiple strategies that frequently open paths to energetically stretched solidarities, connecting issues and people across space and sector. This makes sense, given that the local is never only local, just as the global is also wherever you are reading this book right now. The place-specific horrors of incarceration are also pathways to uprising as well as organizing—from rural hospitals to transportation to bandwidth to borders and beyond. Sustained organizing begins from many starting points, some not yet imagined, and frequently arises from activities not directly connected to criminalization yet directly affected by the aggrandizement of carceral geographies.

As this book makes clear, jails do and do not serve different functions from prisons and detention centers. Even if "prison" has long tended to catch the political and analytical imagination of many of its opponents, jail, like detention, has been right there in the midst of carceral geographies throughout the rise of mass incarceration. These geographies, and the criminalization nourishing their monstrous aggrandizement, grow from the dynamic interplay of ideologies, systems, and outcomes. The simplest phrase to summarize such complexities is "Crime is the problem for which carcerality is the solution." Plenty of researchers have confronted this assumption directly, showing in a variety of ways how it works ideologically to displace curiosity and attention by presenting a self-evident and self-realizing social project.

I and others have revealed the dynamic relationships that characterize the intertwined processes of welfare dismantlement, political criminalization, structural adjustment, domestic militarism, liberation movements, and passive- and counter-revolution against such movements in the USA and beyond. In the context of these multiple upheavals, sometimes initiated from "below," the relative power and relative autonomy of the forces of organized violence consolidated and expanded in the domestic context of crisis and profound restructuring of racial capitalism. The forces of organized violence engage in ongoing restructuring as a significant feature—the institutional and legitimizing embodiments—of the anti-state state. Indeed, in large part they've captured it.

While in many analyses state capture indicates shifting public treasury and public wealth contents into private hands, these chapters show that state capture is also a feature internal to the anti-state state, which has become its own purpose—the purpose of state capture by state agencies is to secure the conditions for the reproduction of those agencies. We can see this in stark assertions of need—whether presented by purveyors of public debt, or local boosters, or uniformed personnel's benevolent associations and unions, or appointed or elected officials justifying their appointments or (re-)election—based in alleged fiduciary responsibility (the language used by the anti-state). We can also see its self-fulfilling purpose in the endless, absolute demand for institutional elaborations—workers, machinery, buildings, rules—to grasp the ever-fleeting objective of a society ordered by "crime." The forces of organized violence imitate, attach, and absorb public welfare missions, while at the same time—in order to legitimize an ever-expanding appetite—herd, constrain, and sacrifice people set into motion by the churn of organized abandonment.

They extract people from lives-in-motion in order to extract time from them. Why time? Because it is the element, become a commodity, that enables flows of carceral cash (wages, debt service, rent, utility bills, vendor invoices, and so on). It is that commodity that inspires, as any system under racial capitalism always will, persistently innovative strategies to direct the flow toward particular coffers: salaries; agency budgets; politicians' reelectability; construction companies and raw materials purveyors; consultants; elite landowners; investment bankers; pension fund bondholders; or other resources that, in the abstract, could be used for anything, but in the ideologically charged ongoing material present, consolidate in the carceral fix.

The commodification of an unfree person's time doesn't end with them being drained of their non-renewable resource, although that is more horror than anyone should bear. As with all carceral interruptions to life-in-motion, unfree persons' households and communities also experience the drain. Not only deprived of time and money resources, they are also exposed to life-shortening effects of powerless worry and ambient toxins that, in sum, contribute to group-differentiated vulnerability to premature death. Monstrous circular and cumulative combinations of ideology and system erupt as outcome in the form of premature death across many demographics.

As is clear in many of this book's cases, a host community's principal justification for feeding some human life-time to the monster is other humans' future—to be secured, according to the prevailing origin-myth, by the monster itself. Hmmm. Let's think about this a bit. First, we see in many cases that a "need" for cages frequently isn't self-evidently a local one; and if it *is* local it stems from the ability of the forces of organized violence to use laws and regulations to fine people into the lockup, using those dollars as revenue to reproduce the capacity to fine the same or similar people into the lockup. Second, we see in other cases, local need having dematerialized—for whatever reasons—that new or enhanced lockups promise future flows of money resources from other treasuries (county, state, or federal). This process persists as long as particularly categorized humans are in custody such that their extracted time can be commodified, thus transformed into the intangible but real medium through which money flows as rent, wages, interest, etc. To make a long story longer: anti-state state-capture relies on human capture to reproduce the conditions of its own reproducibility.

The anti-state state is thus consolidated through provisionally conjoining carceral capacities. What enables this consolidation is, among other things, the exercise of various petty sovereignties. Here we can note a continuum from intimate interpersonal violence, to rape, to lynching, to killer cops, to capital punishment, to war: the violent expression of the right to rule. Organized violence self-legitimates through the threatened and actual disposal of life, interrupting some futures in order to create other futures. Meanwhile, contrary to half-baked political geographic concepts, the local state, in developing or enhancing a jail and employing uniformed personnel, exercises relative sovereignty. That sovereignty is enhanced by the capacity to kill (shoot, lock up in deadly circumstance such as COVID-19 or medical neglect), but also to take on municipal debt in order to construct and maintain the time-extraction/revenue spigot. Debt draws from the future to arrange the present, which means the unchallenged present is, unsurprisingly, the historical geography of the future. (They're planning jails for kids whose parents haven't been born yet.)

Breathtakingly, organized violence's accumulated capacities provoke giddy enthusiasm, summed up by a famous civil rights attorney who declared, "I love the police because all the politicians are afraid of them." Thus, it is probably no wonder that a burgeoning left-fascism "research" agenda insists that "crime" must be solved by more extensive and intensive policing before inalienable means for general social welfare can happen. These presumptive tricks (police! police!) are enabled by and enable the aggrandizing telos of the carceral. They distort what contemporary abolition has persistently been about—as evidenced in organizing, congresses, documents, research, popular publications, and endless hours of podcasts.

Abolition requires we change one thing: everything. *The Jail Is Everywhere*, consisting of cases that stretch across various types of municipalities, partnerships, and urgencies, demonstrates how to know and fight the monstrous carceral, writ large in small bits. Neither riveted by nor cynically familiar with surprise, the protagonists in these cases demonstrate the energetic concentration of creative aggression. They do so by scrutinizing patterned and chance encounters with institutionalized (structural and agential) organized violence, along the way proposing methods for consolidating the capacity of vulnerable people caught in the cascading displacements of organized abandonment. Organized abandonment, and the organized violence grown to maintain and control it, are in sum (whether surprisingly or not) the broad, deep front of a long brutal war. Class war, if you will, shaped by its modalities as race war, gender war, colonial war: the war of racial capitalism against all. This book allows us many powerful, partial views into reworking place, toward making at least an archipelago of historical geographies for abolition's future.

At the end the lessons are always the same: Our backs are to the wall. Be curious. Notice patterns. Start from where you're at. Organize. Study. Read or listen. Share. Organize. *A luta continua.*

New York City
May 15, 2023

Thanks to Lydia Pelot-Hobbs, Jack Norton, Judah Schept, and all the contributors for making this book. And gratitude to comrades I've been thinking with lately, especially Mythri Prasad-Aleyamma, S'bu Zikode, Laura Liu, Mariame Kaba, Kelly Hayes, Siraj Ahmed, Kelly Gillespie, Leigh-Ann Naidoo, Vanessa Thompson, Flávio Almada, Alberto Toscano, Brenna Bhandar, Shellyne Rodriguez, Yvonne Busisiswe Phyllis, Mwelela Cele, Katherine McKittrick, Rosie Warren, Naomi Murakawa, and last, first, and always, Craig Gilmore.

Introduction: The Jail Is Everywhere

Jack Norton, Lydia Pelot-Hobbs, and Judah Schept

There is a quiet jail boom happening across the United States, particularly in the smaller cities and rural counties most often overlooked or mischaracterized by national media. And as county after county has been building bigger and bigger jails, and as more and more people have been detained and incarcerated, the nature of jail incarceration—the way that the different levels of the state are using jails—has changed. Jails are increasingly being used as immigrant detention centers for federal agencies like ICE and the US Marshals. In many states, departments of corrections utilize jails as decentralized state prison systems. And at the county and city level, jails remain a central and expanding infrastructure of the local criminal justice system. When they build it, they fill it, and counties across the country have been building bigger jails and planning for a future of more criminalization, detention, and incarceration.

Whatever the claims of jail boosters, jails are sites of immiseration and death. While jails are often touted by local elites as a necessary response to growing poverty and health disparities, research demonstrates that jail incarceration—and the concentration of resources in sheriff's departments—impoverishes communities and destroys health. Whether they are called jails, detention centers, justice centers, justice campuses, borough-based jails, or county prisons, county and city jails form a diffuse, locally governed network of sites in an ongoing class war in the United States and beyond. They comprise a local and flexible infrastructure for the imposition of austerity, the ongoing entrenchment of state racism, and the reproduction of capitalist social relations, and are an expanding capacity of the carceral state. As the tactics, contingencies, and geography of this war changes, so have the uses of the local jail.

There are over 3,000 counties and parishes in the United States, and almost every one of them has a jail. This fact has been easy to overlook when much of the media and institutional attention on carceral expansion has understandably focused on jails in the largest cities, and on federal and state prison siting. County jail incarceration is rising fastest outside of major cities, and rural and suburban counties have been sinking vast sums of public debt to construct new and bigger jails. One of the central challenges of movement-building to meet this expansion of carceral capacity is precisely its decentralized and local nature. The jail is everywhere, and people have been fighting back against incarceration and criminalization in communities across the country. Often these fights have been seen—and even experienced—as local or provincial, rather than as key struggles for abolitionist futures at the center points of a new geography of mass incarceration.

Unlike state or federal prisons, jails are for the most part built, owned, and operated by county or city governments, and are used to incarcerate or detain people pretrial for relatively short periods of time. County jails, however, are not on the margins of the carceral state. Nearly every person imprisoned in the US first spends time in a jail, and in recent decades the jail has become much more than a place to detain the local "rabble," as John Irwin, in one of the foundational studies of the American jail, wrote in 1985. In the nearly four decades since Irwin's *The Jail*—a book published in the midst of the largest prison expansion in US history—the number of people incarcerated or detained in local jails on any given day in the United States has increased nearly threefold, in part due to the shifting role of the jail as a site of coherence for policing, state and federal prisons, and immigrant detention.

Jails today house people pretrial and for sentences under a year in most states, and under three to five years in others. Some states have taken advantage of bipartisan prison reform efforts of the last decade to lower prison populations. While this has reduced the overall number of people incarcerated in some places, such as California, in others, including Kentucky, Tennessee, and Indiana, it has simply shifted carceral power and capacity downscale to the jail. Counties across the country face the pressures of more people sentenced to felonies being sent to jail, and they build bigger jails in the face of this pressure, almost always at the urging of the sheriff's office and with the encouragement of jail architects and consultants, and even federal judges. At the same time, there are incentives for counties to expand local jail capacity to try and capture revenue from state and federal agencies. Whatever the combination of pressures and incentives, local jails have become a key site of carceral power and expansion and continue to be central to racial capitalist development and planning efforts across the rural to urban spectrum.

While the jail is everywhere, there has also been a significant geographical shift in local incarceration. In mid-year 2019, there were an estimated 758,420 people in local jails, 31,000 more than in mid-year 2013. During that time, jail incarceration in the largest cities in the US dropped 18 percent, while jail incarceration in rural counties increased 27 percent. These numbers represent real people—hundreds of thousands of people who are directly impacted by the violence of jail incarceration and detention, millions of people who are affected by the extraction that jail facilitates, and by the violence that is perpetrated on families and communities through policing and incarceration across the varied geography of the United States.[1]

---

1 Jacob Kang-Brown et al., *People in Jail in 2019* (New York: Vera Institute of Justice, December 2019).

3

This is a book about how everyday people are organizing against the expansion of jail infrastructures in their communities as a front line of struggles against mass incarceration. Cities and counties are building huge jails in new places and new jails in the same places. In their organizing, activists are confronting the rise of carceral humanism, the devolution of state prison systems to jails, and federal agencies contracting with sheriff's departments. Drawing on progressive arguments about improving conditions of confinement and enhancing people's rehabilitation, county and city officials are positioning jails as sites of care. In doing so, they reinscribe notions of certain racialized, classed, and gendered people as in need of "fixing" while obfuscating the fundamental dehumanization and violence of the cage. At the same time, organizers are confronting county and city officials returning to the same tired arguments of prison boosters—false promises that jails will solve their political economic problems. And in the face of austerity and a relentless political commitment to incarceration and detention, organizers are finding that their jail fights are not so local, as the forces they are confronting are produced by the devolution of state and federal imprisonment.

Carceral Humanism

In a 2006 article, the organizer Rose Braz keenly observed that plans for another round of prison expansion in California had abandoned the language of "tough on crime."[2] Instead, the administration of Arnold Schwarzenegger, then the governor, couched the proposal for almost a hundred new facilities of varying security levels in the idiom of "prison reform" and, more specifically, "gender responsiveness." Just a few years

2 Rose Braz, "Kinder, Gentler, Gender Responsive Cages: Prison Expansion Is Not Prison Reform," *Women, Girls and Criminal Justice* (October/November 2006): 87–91.

later, other organizers began fighting jail expansion efforts in other communities around the country that bore a striking resemblance to what Braz first observed in California, namely the justification for massive carceral growth in the language of human rights, therapeutic justice, and reform.[3] James Kilgore, whose chapter in this volume details the fight against jail expansion in Champaign-Urbana, Illinois, coined the phrase "carceral humanism" to describe what at that time in 2014 felt like an emerging logic of incarceration.[4] Ten years later, as this book goes to print, carceral humanism is a central tendency of arguments for jail growth.

As the chapters in this volume make clear, Braz's analysis of expansion through appeals to a "kinder, gentler" incarceration has proved prescient. Many of the authors here name carceral humanism and its constitutive features as central to jail expansion efforts in their communities. What, exactly, does carceral humanism mean, why has it become so important to jail expansion efforts, and how are organizers finding ways to fight it?

Carceral humanism is a new expression of an older argument. While incarceration has always been wielded as a class-war project, it hasn't only relied on punitive attitudes for credibility.[5] There is also a historical legacy of prisons as reform projects, where proponents justified incarceration around principles of rehabilitation and treatment, often through paternalistic ideas of extending notions of American exceptionalism to racialized

---

3 James Kilgore, "Repackaging Mass Incarceration," *CounterPunch*, June 6, 2014; Judah Schept, *Progressive Punishment: Job Loss, Jail Growth, and the Neoliberal Logic of Carceral Expansion* (New York: New York University Press, 2015).

4 Kilgore, "Repackaging Mass Incarceration."

5 Ruth Wilson Gilmore, *Abolition Geography: Essays Towards Liberation* (New York: Verso, 2022); Peter Linebaugh, *Stop, Thief!: The Commons, Enclosures, and Resistance* (Oakland, CA: PM Press, 2014); Jarrod Shananan and Zhandarka Kurti, *States of Incarceration: Rebellion, Reform, and America's Punishment System* (London: Reaktion Books, 2022).

subjects and bringing or restoring them to idealized notions of wage labor productivity.[6] The historian David Rothman has pointedly argued that reform efforts "may well have done less to upgrade dismal conditions than they did to create nightmares of their own."[7]

What, then, distinguishes today's carceral humanism from these older approaches? First, contemporary attempts to collapse welfare and treatment into incarceration reflect a very different historical conjuncture. Half a century of harshly punitive and racist criminal justice policy, the mass imprisonment it has enabled, and the exponential growth in the number of prisons and jails in the United States have built out carceral capacities across every scale of the state. This has occurred in the same historical moment as deindustrialization, austerity, and heightened inequality. Second, in recent decades, an emergent if shallow multicultural and bipartisan criminal justice reform effort has materialized, the efforts of which have shrunk some state prison populations through incremental legislative fixes, while often shoring up the legitimacy of incarceration overall, at times through devolution (i.e., moving people from a prison to a jail) rather than decarceration (i.e., getting people out). In the context of both neoliberal abandonment and state devolution, the jail is increasingly the catchall "solution" to every social problem.[8] For well-meaning city officials, concerned by mass incarceration but also by unaffordable housing, unemployment,

---

6 Angela Y. Davis, *Are Prisons Obsolete?* (New York: Seven Stories Press, 2003); Michel Foucault, *Discipline and Punish: The Birth of the Prison* (New York: Vintage Books, 1995); David Garland, *Punishment and Modern Society: A Study in Social Theory* (Chicago: University of Chicago Press, 1990); David Rothman, *Conscience and Convenience: The Asylum and Its Alternatives in Progressive America* (New York: De Gruyter 2002).

7 Rothman, *Conscience and Convenience*, 9.

8 Ruth Wilson Gilmore and Craig Gilmore, "Beyond Bratton," in *Policing the Planet: Why the Policing Crisis Led to Black Lives Matter*, ed. Jordan T. Camp and Christina Heatherton (New York: Verso, 2016).

6

addiction, and lack of treatment options, the jail has become a way to imagine doing incarceration differently, including as a mechanism to extend important services to marginalized populations. Understanding this moment as an expression of carceral humanism is thus both a periodizing and political maneuver, naming the ways that jails (and other elements of the carceral state) are recast as social (and indeed "social justice") services in a long historical moment defined by organized violence as a solution to the problems produced by organized abandonment.[9]

The chapters in this volume offer crucial and expansive insight into the different ways that carceral humanism manifests in different geographic and political contexts. Moreover, they demonstrate that this new central tendency of expansion constitutes far more than just an ideological shift in the justifications for imprisonment but rather emerges out of material conditions in the United States and can mobilize powerful material resources. In Sacramento, officials and attorneys interpreted a consent decree focused on the current jail's violation of both the Americans with Disabilities Act (ADA) and the Health Insurance Portability and Accountability Act (HIPAA) as greenlighting a new jail construction project, arguing a new jail was the best way to meet the needs of people with disabilities (Blum, this volume). Similarly, in New Orleans, federal judges placed a consent decree on the jail because of poor conditions and threatened City Council members with contempt of court—including fines and possible jail time—if they did not move forward with new jail construction (Peterson-Burge, this volume). A central lesson from those fights—that conditions of confinement and class action lawsuits and judicial approaches toward reducing overcrowding or addressing poor conditions can result in *increases* to carceral capacity—should caution anti-jail activists as they consider various tactics. Many communities position new jails

---

9 Gilmore, *Abolition Geography*.

as mechanisms through which to increase access to a variety of mental and physical health services, poverty programs, and substance abuse treatment programs for residents (Heiss, this volume; Kilgore, this volume; Pragasz and Revier, this volume). In other places, critics of incarceration who occupy powerful positions in universities, foundations, city governments, and nonprofit organizations, propose and design new facilities presumed to meet the needs of women and gender-expansive people (Mohapatra, this volume), one of many examples of an emergent liberal/progressive counterinsurgency against abolitionist demands.[10] In still other places, new jails are proposed as expressions of city commitments to racial justice (Bervera and Ware, this volume). Finally, in one conservative district, Republican lawmakers deployed a communications strategy reliant on the notions of humane and service-oriented jailing in order to win the consent of liberals to a jail-building proposal (Westover and Witt, this volume).

There are thousands of jails in the United States, through which more than 10 million people cycle each year. People affected by jail—all people—should have access to education and treatment; institutions should absolutely be accessible for people with all kinds of disabilities and should absolutely be able to respond to and provide care for women, trans, and nonbinary people in ways that affirm their gender identities and needs. Carceral humanism, however, is primarily an appeal for greater carceral capacity; as these chapters make clear, no one is safer inside a jail cell.

---

10 Dylan Rodríguez and Roberto Sirvent, "Insurgency and Counterinsurgency: An Interview with Dylan Rodríguez," *Black Agenda Report*, November 2, 2022. See also Orisanmi Burton, *Tip of the Spear: Black Radicalism, Prison Repression, and the Long Attica Revolt* (Berkeley: University of California Press, 2023), and Shanahan and Kurti, *States of Incarceration*.

Devolution of State Prison Systems to Jails

In recent years, dozens of state governments have shuttered prisons from California to Florida, Colorado to New York. According to the Sentencing Project, states' capacity to cage has dropped by 81,444 prison beds between 2000 and 2022.[11] This unprecedented reduction in prison bed space during the era of mass incarceration has been due to a mix of organizing by decarceration activists, state fiscal contractions, and federal court mandates.

Yet frequently missing from this story is the extent to which states are turning to county and city jails to incarcerate state prisoners. At year end 2021 (the most recent data as of this writing), 64,648 state prisoners were held in local jails—6.2 percent of all state prisoners. While at first glance this number might not seem noteworthy, when further examined a pattern emerges. Thirteen states hold 80 percent of the national population of state prisoners in local jails—overwhelmingly in the South. Arkansas, Georgia, Kentucky, Louisiana, Mississippi, Tennessee, Utah, and Virginia all incarcerate more than 10 percent of their state prison populations in jails, with Kentucky and Louisiana each incarcerating nearly half of their state prisoners in county or parish jails.[12]

What is happening here?

A number of factors have converged to produce this devolution. While sheriff's departments are frequently identified as the primary propellers of this carceral realignment, multiple factors have made this arrangement not only feasible but desirable. On one hand, federal courts' mandating prison population limits in the face of overcrowding and conditions of confinement lawsuits have compelled states to find or make more bed

---

11 The Sentencing Project, "Repurposing Correctional Facilities to Strengthen Communities," August 2022, sentencingproject.org.

12 E. Ann Carson. "Prisoners in 2021—Statistical Tables," Bureau of Justice Statistics, December 2022, bjs.ojp.gov.

space. At the same time, neoliberal restructuring has involved fiscal austerity for many state and local governments. While for state officials incarcerating someone in a jail serves as a solution insofar as it is cheaper than building new prisons, for certain county and municipal officials, jail expansion comes to be seen as a fix for endemic political economic crises. It is in this context that sheriffs mobilize and organize to expand their jails and their punitive power bloc. This interplay of state forces completely sidelines the possibility of decarceration or decriminalization as a legitimate political objective.

This dynamic first developed in a piecemeal fashion in Louisiana over the course of the 1970s to the 1990s. In the face of an extensive conditions-of-confinement lawsuit, federal courts placed population limits on the Louisiana State Penitentiary—and sheriffs were forced to hold state prisoners in their jails. In response to sheriffs' ire at shouldering this additional cost, the Louisiana state legislature innovated a new policy in 1976: a per diem system where the state department of corrections would allocate to sheriffs' departments a certain amount of money per state prisoner held each night in a parish jail. This carceral arrangement was initially understood as a temporary stopgap while the state built new prisons. But sheriffs began to see this arrangement as beneficial insofar as per diem monies increased their economic and political resources—leading sheriffs to band together to organize against state prison building and for more state prisoners in their jails. By the 1990s, this had become a permanent solution, with the incarceration of half of Louisiana's prisoners in jails across the state.[13]

By the turn of the twenty-first century, other states began implementing their own cooperation agreements between state corrections departments and county sheriffs' departments. During the 1990s, state-sentenced prisoners in the South and

---

13 Lydia Pelot-Hobbs, *Prison Capital: Mass Incarceration and Struggles for Abolition Democracy in Louisiana*, (Chapel Hill: University of North Carolina Press, 2023).

parts of the Midwest increasingly found themselves doing time in a jail.[14] These policies were further extended in 2011 when the US Supreme Court ruled that the overcrowding of the California prison system constituted cruel and unusual punishment *and* that California was prohibited from building new prisons to rectify overcrowding. In response, California policymakers instituted what they termed "realignment," or relying on county jails to manage overcrowding pressures.[15] What had once been a rarity in the carceral landscape was becoming commonplace.

This carceral devolution is a geographic form of state restructuring that concentrates resources in sheriffs' offices. It is important to keep in mind that in many rural and suburban locales, the sheriff's office is one of the most powerful elected political offices, responsible for overseeing the jail, along with serving as the county's police force and tax collectors. The funneling of per diem revenue payments further increases their power. Sheriffs are unable to pocket surplus revenue for their own personal enrichment, but they do have discretion on *how* these monies are spent, with little to no oversight. Generally speaking, they direct the bare minimum of per diem payments to any semblance of incarcerated people's well-being. Instead, these monies are usually allotted to increasing jail staff, purchasing new punitive equipment, and, at times, jail renovations. New technologies and shiny renovations further the notion that sheriffs can make jails humane through modernization projects. Furthermore, the hiring of more sheriff's deputies is routinely leveraged to build consent for the sheriff's office. Deputies have been known to spend their time supporting public works projects from cleaning up parks to coordinating meals for the

---

14 Paul Guerino, Paige M. Harrison, and William J. Sabol, "Prisoners in 2010," Bureau of Justice Statistics, February 9, 2012, bjs.ojp.gov.

15 Nancy Heitzeg and Kay Whitlock, "Prison Reform, Proposition 47 and the California Shell Game," *Prison Legal News*, March 31, 2017, prisonlegalnews.org.

elderly. In doing so, sheriffs ingratiate themselves with residents who will go to the polls to keep a sheriff in office (or not). Which is to say, the carceral per diem revenue system shores up and expands sheriffs' jailing fiefdoms while incentivizing sheriffs to lock up more and more state prisoners in their jails.

Sheriffs advocating to expand their jails rely on a mix of financing techniques. Most of these techniques are the same ones used for expanding their jails for pretrial prisoners and those sentenced to county or municipal time. The most common funding strategy is asking voters to approve new property taxes to cover the cost of multi-year loans for jail expansions. However, it is not uncommon for residents to vote down these proposals due to a mix of anti-jail organizing and generalized anti-tax sentiment. In response, some localities have attempted to sidestep voter opposition by borrowing a tactic from prison expansion—the use of lease revenue bonds (LRBs) for new jail construction. As Liz Blum notes in her discussion of jailing in Sacramento, LRBs "allow governments to expedite major construction projects by removing the requirement of voter approval and are one of the most expensive loans a county can receive."[16] Through funneling tax dollars via various loopholes, creditors are enriched while residents are disenfranchised, all to intensify criminalizing regimes.[17] One devolution-financing tactic that differs from general jail expansion strategies is the state legislatures' creation of programs whereby the state will subsidize jail expansions in return for sheriffs committing to holding a percentage of their bed space for state prisoners.

It is important to note that this devolution process would not be possible if it weren't also attractive to state and local officials. While federal judges have prompted this realignment

---

16 Liz Blum, "Decarcerating Sacramento: Confronting Jail Expansion in California's Capital," p. 59 in this volume.

17 For more on lease revenue bonds see Ruth Wilson Gilmore, *Golden Gulag: Prisons, Surplus, Crisis, and Opposition in Globalizing California* (Berkeley: University of California Press, 2007).

of state prison systems, governors and state legislators have passed laws and created mechanisms to facilitate this carceral configuration. For them this arrangement meets various economic and political needs. As neoliberalism has delegitimized raising taxes and promoted the adoption of tight debt ceilings in the name of the "anti-state state," elected officials have diminished state revenues to work with.[18] While departments of corrections have been one of the few areas prioritized, mass imprisonment is still a costly affair. The lack of political will to meaningfully move away from punitive politics in response to overcrowding means elected officials are unwilling to turn to early release or decriminalization as a solution. Locking up state prisoners in jails maintains the centrality of incarceration while saving state dollars. Not only are per diem payments on average much lower than the annual cost per day of incarcerating someone in a prison, but it is even cheaper than taking out debt to finance new prison construction. And even when state legislatures create programs to aid sheriffs in expanding their jails for warehousing state prisoners, the debt does not impact the state's bond rating as it is officially taken on by the county.

For local governments, the expansion of their county jails is frequently seen as an opportunity to manage their own political and economic problems. The slashing of federal revenue-sharing programs and state cuts to localities have translated to fiscal crises for counties across the country. Rural counties and smaller cities and suburbs have been hit particularly hard as these cuts have been joined by deindustrialization and shrinking tax bases. In the context of budget tightening and limited political vision, local leaders often back jail expansion as a needed job creation program for struggling communities. And for the jurisdictions where the sheriff is contracting with the department of corrections, per diem payments buoy the sheriff

18 Ruth Wilson Gilmore and Craig Gilmore, "Restating the Obvious," in *Indefensible Space: The Architecture of the National Security State,* ed. Michael Sorkin (New York: Routledge, 2007).

department's budget—allowing less revenue to be allocated toward jail operations.

Jails, ICE, and US Marshals

These state-county devolution dynamics are mirrored in federal agencies' contracting with jails. As Silky Shah documents in her chapter "County Jails and the Immigrant Dragnet," jails have become enmeshed in immigration detention and deportation. Following President Ronald Reagan making the detainment of unauthorized migrants mandatory in the early 1980s, federal immigration enforcement (first Immigration and Naturalization Service and then Immigration and Customs Enforcement) have contracted with hundreds of local jails to incarcerate immigrants.[19] And while the federal government has expanded its archipelago of federal immigration detention facilities, jails continue to be a more cost-effective option. As in the devolution of the state prison system, ICE pays a per diem to sheriff's departments for immigrant detainees, albeit at a much higher rate than state prison systems. This has incentivized sheriffs to fill their cells with immigrants awaiting deportation hearings. Under these conditions, localities end up politically invested in racist and draconian immigration policies under the false premise that jailing immigrants will solve their fiscal woes.[20]

Moreover, jails have become yet another site of immigration policing. Sheriffs routinely consent to ICE holds or holding someone suspected of being undocumented beyond their official

---

19 Jonathan Simon, "Refugees in a Carceral Age: The Rebirth of Immigration Prisons in the United States," *Public Culture* 10, no. 3 (1998): 579–83; Michael Welch, *Detained: Immigration Laws and the Expanding I.N.S. Jail Complex* (Philadelphia: Temple University Press, 2002).

20 Jacob Kang-Brown and Jack Norton, "More than a Jail: Immigrant Detention and the Smell of Money," *In Our Backyards Stories*, July 5, 2018, vera.org.

Figure 1: Local Jails Providing Federal Detention, 2013–19
Jacob Kang-Brown, 2023. Data source: Bureau of Justice Statistics.

release date (from their bail being paid or their case being over) in order for ICE to run their citizenship information. Sheriff's deputies' everyday involvement in detention and deportation is particularly severe in places that have entered 287(g) agreements —the deputization of local law enforcement to act as immigration enforcement. For cities and counties where the sheriffs are the police, this creates the situation where the sheriff's department simultaneously operates as border police and immigrant detention.[21]

The use of county jails for federal pretrial detention by the United States Marshals Service (USMS) has also served as a pull factor for many exurban counties building larger facilities since the mid-1980s. Federal crime bills increased federal caseloads significantly, nearly doubling them, for example, in the first decade following the Comprehensive Crime Control Act of 1984. As more and more people were detained pretrial for the federal government, USMS began to establish and expand

---

21 Oliver Hinds and Jack Norton, "No Chance Alamance: Immigrant Detention and Jail Expansion in the North Carolina Piedmont," *In Our Backyards Stories*, July 28, 2020, vera.org.

a network of county jails, often in rural counties, where they could detain people in exchange for per diem payments. Most contracts that counties sign with USMS for use of local jails also allow for immigration detention, and per diem payments from ICE. Payments from these federal agencies—and even just the promise of such payments—has in many cases given sheriffs and other county officials political leverage to build larger jails. This in turn has led to an "intercounty carceral arms race" as counties vie to "rent beds" to ICE, USMS, state corrections departments, and neighboring counties.[22]

Jail Is Class War

There is a long tradition of analysis and political activity that understands policing and incarceration as instruments of class war. Intellectuals writing in the Marxist tradition have centered cops and cages in their analyses of the ongoing primitive accumulation of capital—domestically and abroad—and to "structuring the accumulation of capital, controlling public space, [and] regulating labor relations."[23] Ruth Wilson Gilmore has written extensively on how incarceration, and the United

---

22 Jack Norton and Jacob Kang-Brown, "If You Build It: How the Federal Government Fuels Jail Expansion," *In Our Backyards Stories*, January 10, 2020, vera.org. For more on the Comprehensive Crime Control Bill of 1984, see David Stein, "The Untold Story: Joe Biden Pushed Ronald Reagan to Ramp Up Incarceration—Not the Other Way Around," theintercept.com, September 17, 2019.

23 Jack Norton and David Stein, "Materializing Race: On Capitalism and Mass Incarceration," *Spectre Magazine*, October 22, 2020, spectrejournal.com. See also David Correia and Tyler Wall, *Police: A Field Guide* (New York: Verso, 2018); Peter Linebaugh, *The London Hanged: Crime and Civil Society in the Eighteenth Century* (New York: Verso, 2016); Tony Platt et al., *The Iron Fist and the Velvet Glove: An Analysis of the U.S. Police* (San Francsico: Crime and Social Justice Associates, 1977).

States prison boom around the turn of the century, is "official racial class war," part of the "abandonment of one set of public mandates in favor of another—of social welfare to domestic warfare."[24] Orisanmi Burton, in his study of the long Attica revolt in New York State, argues that "prisons are war," and are "state strategies of race war, class war, colonization, and counterinsurgency."[25] These analyses extend to the jail. As John Irwin noted, the jail "was devised as, and continues to be, the special social device for controlling ... the lowest class of people"[26] While the uses and capacities of jails have been shifting and expanding around the country, and the jail is a part of a larger, expansive carceral state capacity, jails are still locally controlled, and jail construction is still happening at the scale of the county, city, or region. As these chapters make clear, class war is all around us, and the jail is everywhere.

As the carceral state's capacities have shifted and reorganized around jails, organizers have had to shift their focus as well. There have been campaigns against new or expanded jails in large cities like New York, Los Angeles, and Atlanta; in midsize cities like New Orleans, Indianapolis, and Oklahoma City; and in dozens of small towns and rural counties around the country. And while there is some coordination and communication between and among these fights, these struggles can also remain isolated from each other and from broader movements. As such, there is also a dearth of information and analysis identifying key points of distinction and leverage when it comes to fighting jail expansion, including issues of funding, revenue, and multi-jurisdictional incarceration. We hope that this volume, which brings together a range of knowledge and experience from jail fights across the country, can help map not only this new terrain of the carceral state, but also the

---

24 Gilmore, *Golden Gulag*, 64; Gilmore, *Abolition Geography*, 338.
25 Burton, *Tip of the Spear*.
26 John Irwin, *The Jail: Managing the Underclass in American Society* (Berkeley: University of California Press, 2013), 3.

emergent abolitionist opposition, by foregrounding the hard-forged analyses of anti-jail organizers themselves, as they take us through their seemingly local fights, which are actually at the center of the carceral state.

1

A Quiet Jail Boom

Jasmine Heiss

In 2017, I joined the Vera Institute to help lead the newly launched In Our Backyards Initiative, a project meant to understand and confront the rise of jail incarceration in smaller cities and rural communities. The project was anchored by Vera researcher and criminologist Jacob Kang-Brown's county-level analysis of jail and prison incarceration data, which revealed a quiet but dramatic shift in the geography of local incarceration. While incarceration rates in major cities began to decline in the late 1990s, less populous communities have continued to lock people up at increasingly higher rates. Rural counties now have the highest rates of jail incarceration in the country, followed by smaller cities. These communities also have deep and persistent racial disparities in criminalization and incarceration and have driven the recent rise in women's incarceration.

Jack Norton joined the project shortly before me and was at the time finishing a PhD at the CUNY Graduate Center. Jack worked on the project as a field researcher, investigating the social, economic, and political context of small, high-incarceration communities and the experiences of people who live there. As our shared work over the ensuing five years made clear, the new geography of mass incarceration is both facilitated and precipitated by resource concentration in jails and supervision. In a context of yawning inequality and the evisceration of state and local budgets, abetted by right-wing anti-tax movements, the political choices that shape high-incarceration communities are often obscured by a narrative of inevitability and decline. Hospitals close, jails expand. Crime and punishment, the story goes, are things that happen to nameless, faceless people in certain kinds of places.

The central focus of In Our Backyards, accordingly, grew beyond research to include shifting power and resources to people organizing against expanding jails and criminalization in smaller cities and rural communities. Hundreds of local jail fights have been waged in the past decade, often repeatedly in the same community. We worked alongside local organizers and in state legislatures to limit the criminalization and punishment of poor and marginalized people and to re-politicize the policy choices that render people disposable. Ultimately, this work was not just in service of implementing discrete policy interventions. Rather, it was an effort to expand understanding about the new geography of incarceration and moral imagination about what it might mean to live in a world without jails.

For the past few decades, to discuss the geography of incarceration in the United States was to talk about a sort of banishment to the rural hinterland. The prison boom that spanned the early 1970s to the 1990s saw people—particularly Black men —exiled from the nation's biggest cities and sentenced to live in state and federal prisons in isolated and often-desperate places. As both the length and number of sentences increased, the story goes, newly minted prison towns embraced the rapid expansion of the prison-industrial complex as deliverance from economic decline.

For example, in 2018, a description of the effort to build a new federal prison in Letcher County, Kentucky, evoked themes of both spiritual redemption and bootstrap capitalism. Under the heading, "Prison as Salvation," an NBC news reporter wrote, "Letcher County's bid to be the home of America's next federal prison stems from its willingness to try something, anything, to save itself."[1] Central to this logic is an understanding of the prison-industrial complex as an equation in which prosperity is extracted from poor, mostly Black communities, and transferred primarily to white people in deindustrialized cities and rural communities where prisons are sited.

The real story is much more complicated. First, the nation's prison towns are not a hegemonic sea of whiteness. They include communities in the Mississippi Delta, in the forested hills of Arkansas, and on the edge of the Chihuahuan Desert in southern New Mexico. The anti-state state project of prison building, as Ruth Wilson Gilmore reminds us, is a race-making project, but not necessarily some formulaic transfer of wealth from Black to white, or urban to rural communities. Rather, "the two locations are joined in a constant churn of unacknowledged though shared precarious desperation."[2] Incarceration and policing is often the only "fix" on offer for social crises across the urban-to-rural spectrum.

Understanding the new geography of mass incarceration in the United States also demands a wider lens, and a greater attention to scale. Focusing solely on state and federal prisons as the sites that reveal urban and rural communities' shared precarity obscures the most ubiquitous form of carceral infrastructure: the local jail. In Letcher County, due in large part to tenacious abolitionist organizing, no new federal prison has yet been built. But the fifty-four-bed local jail in the county regularly holds well over 100 people, the majority of whom are either sitting behind bars because they can't pay bail, awaiting hearings after allegedly violating their probation or other forms of supervision, or serving sentences for misdemeanor

---

1 Jon Schuppe, "Does America Need Another Prison?," nbcnews. com, March 22, 2018.

2 Ruth Wilson Gilmore, "Prisons and Class Warfare, An Interview with Clément Petitjean/Période," in *Abolition Geography, Essays Towards Liberation*, ed. Brenna Bhandar and Alberto Toscano (New York: Verso, 2022), 374.

convictions.[3] In county jails across the country, the criminal legal system's most mundane cruelty is on display.

Both a cause and consequence of jail incarceration's continued growth is increased investment in new and larger jails, a phenomenon that we started calling the "quiet jail boom."[4] Most states have not built new prisons in recent decades, and only a handful of states seem poised to break ground on new facilities in coming years. In contrast, the number of jail beds increased 35 percent between 2000 and 2020.[5] This has meant a jail construction boom of new or expanded jails that has taken place primarily outside of the nation's biggest cities, in places like Colorado's San Juan Valley, California's Central Valley, southwest Georgia, and throughout Appalachia.[6]

When we began to try to understand this problem in the wake of the 2016 presidential election, national pundits were already scrutinizing so-called "deaths of despair" in rural communities.[7] In this context, the go-to explanation of both law enforcement and well-meaning reformers was to blame the opioid epidemic and widespread methamphetamine abuse for

---

3 See "Kentucky Department of Corrections Weekly Jail Reports," corrections.ky.gov.

4 Jasmine Heiss and Jack Norton, "The Hidden Scandal of US Criminal Justice? Rural Incarceration Has Boomed," theguardian.com, December 13, 2019.

5 See Allen J. Beck and Jennifer C. Karberg, *Prison and Jail Inmates at Midyear 2000* (Washington, DC: US Department of Justice, March 2001), and Zhen Zeng, *Jail Inmates in 2021* (Washington, DC: US Department of Justice, December 2022). At midyear 2000, the rated capacity of the nation's local jails was estimated at 677,787. By midyear 2020, the rated capacity was 913,700 beds.

6 See Jack Norton, "Life and Jail in Southern Colorado: Alamosa and Pueblo Counties," *In Our Backyards Stories*, April 19, 2018, vera. org; Jacob Kang-Brown and Jack Norton, "Funding Jail Expansion in California's Central Valley," October 8, 2020, vera.org.

7 Maggie Fox, "Where 'Despair Deaths' Were Higher, Voters Chose Trump," nbcnews.com, September 5, 2018.

rising jail incarcerations.[8] This framing is politically convenient in that it divorces the problem of increasing local incarceration from policy and investment decisions, tying it instead to individual failure or deviance that needs to be managed or disciplined by the state. As Naomi Murakawa argues in her examination of the racial construction of the methamphetamine epidemic, "when health problems are constructed as problems of individual behavior, as has been the case with obesity, tobacco, and drug abuse, then political accounts put a premium on criticizing individuals rather than larger determinants of health."[9] Given that incarceration is consistently associated with an increase in drug-related harm, including overdose death, this logic is particularly perverse.[10] The jails built to "save" drug users from themselves contribute to their premature deaths.

The small-city and rural jail boom is better understood as the fallout of a fragmented social safety net, the hollowing out of industry, and a state project that has embraced carceral institutions as the only legitimate manifestation of care. In this context, criminalization and jail incarceration becomes a required experience for marginalized people who need access

8 See, for example, Norton, "Life and Jail in Southern Colorado," for a discussion of efforts to expand the Pueblo County jail; Ohio's state-funded jail-building project justified in the name of building treatment capacity as announced by Governor Mike DeWine in "Governor DeWine Announces Renovation, Repurposing of Former Hocking County Prison," December 13, 2021, governor.ohio.gov.

9 Naomi Murakawa, "Toothless: The Methamphetamine 'Epidemic,' 'Meth Mouth,' and the Racial Construction of Drug Scares," *Du Bois Review* 8, no. 1 (2011): 219–28.

10 See Evan Wood et al., "Recent Incarceration Independently Associated with Syringe Sharing by Injection Drug Users," *Public Health Reports* 120, no. 2 (March–April 2005):150–6; Ingrid A. Binswanger et al., "Release from Prison—A High Risk of Death for Former Inmates," *New England Journal of Medicine* 356, no. 2 (February 2007): 157–65; Elias Nosrati et al., "Economic Decline, Incarceration, and Mortality from Drug Use Disorders in the USA Between 1983 and 2014: An Observational Analysis," *Lancet Public Health* 4, no.7 (2019), e326–33.

to resources or services. Every new social problem, including but not limited to substance use, becomes a problem to be managed by local judges and jailers. Writer and activist James Kilgore has called this repackaging "carceral humanism," a phenomenon in which punishment is recast as social service and all resources that might otherwise strengthen and serve communities are collapsed into the jail.

Drug courts have also flourished in this landscape alongside an ever-expanding number of other "problem-solving" or specialty courts. Rather than untethering social supports from incarceration, drug courts and other specialty courts reinforce the mediation of treatment through the legal system, often with the requirement of a plea, and then subject people to increased jail time for breaking often draconian rules created by judges and other justice system actors who have no medical training, but act as self-appointed experts on recovery and psychology.[11] As the number of women in local jails has increased over the past several decades, local justice systems have also taken on the responsibility of managing familial relationships and the appropriate performance of parenthood. For example, analysis of the Early County, Georgia, jail population showed that after motor-vehicle or traffic-related charges and drug charges, the third most prevalent charge bringing people to jail was against parents whose children were not enrolled in or were not attending school, a violation of Georgia's mandatory education statute.[12] Elsewhere, eugenicist judges have offered jail credits to people who agree to undergo vasectomies or submit to other forms of birth control. When reprimanding one Tennessee judge

---

11 For a discussion on the failures of drug courts in the United States, see Christine Mehta, *Neither Justice Nor Treatment: Drug Courts in the United States* (New York: Physicians for Human Rights, June 2017); Drugs, Security and Democracy Program, *Drug Courts in the Americas* (New York: Social Science Research Council, October 2018).

12 Rural Jails Research Hub, *Early County, GA Jail Trends* (Atlanta: University of Georgia, March 2022).

for coercing people into invasive medical procedures, the Tennessee Board of Judicial Conduct noted that he was trying to accomplish a "worthy goal in preventing the birth of substance addicted babies."[13]

Even prior to the current Supreme Court's evisceration of the right to bodily autonomy, abortion was effectively inaccessible in much of the country, particularly in high-incarceration rural communities. In a post-*Roe* United States with an expanding local carceral infrastructure, one can imagine the logical outgrowth of this phenomenon to be the mass criminalization of people seeking abortion, and of those who aid them. It is also foreseeable that the wages of this zealotry will be premature death and deepening inequities in reproductive health, particularly for Black mothers and children in high-incarceration counties, given that increases in Black incarceration are associated with higher risk of preterm birth among Black women.[14]

Central to the creation and maintenance of the jail boom and the logic of punishment-as-care that has helped sustain it is the nearly unfettered discretion that local judges and law enforcement enjoy. In every major struggle to reduce criminal penalties, pretrial detention or arrests, police, judges, and prosecutors fight to retain the ability to arrest and detain—sometimes indefinitely—anyone who they believe should be under state control. Investments in new and bigger jails across the country are ultimately investments in deepening class oppression and relationships of subjugation. This plays out at the county and

---

13 The Tennessee Board of Judicial Conduct to the Honorable Sam Benningfield, "Board of Judicial Conduct Complaints: File Nos. B17-7052, B17-7055 and B17-7144," public letter of reprimand, November 15, 2017, tncourts.gov; American Civil Liberties Union, "Judge Imposes Birth Control to Prevent Michigan Woman from Having More Children," press release, July 8, 2003, aclu.org.

14 Lauren Dyer et al., "Mass Incarceration and Public Health: The Association Between Black Jail Incarceration and Adverse Birth Outcomes among Black Women in Louisiana," *BMC Pregnancy and Childbirth* 19, no. 1 (2019): 525.

municipal level, where court and jail fines, as well as costs and fees, further immiserate criminalized people while offsetting court and sheriff budgets.

In contrast, struggles against jail construction and for jail closure allow us to refigure the relationship between urban and rural incarceration. If people experience shared precarity across place, place-based organizing against jail construction and for jail closures also has the potential to create a sense of mutual destiny and a shared commitment to questioning the fundamental legitimacy of jails. Shared experiences of criminalization and abandonment become fertile ground from which to imagine and grow a new world. As new technologies of punishment proliferate, with the tentacles of monitoring, surveillance, and supervision extending beyond the jail and more deeply into communities, expansive movement building is increasingly urgent.

2

The Long Fight Against Jail Expansion in Champaign-Urbana, Illinois

An Interview with James Kilgore of Build Programs Not Jails

James Kilgore is an activist, researcher, and writer based in Urbana, Illinois, where he has lived since being paroled from prison in 2009. He is the founder of the Challenging E-Carceration project at MediaJustice and the director of advocacy and outreach for FirstFollowers Reentry Program in Champaign, Illinois. He was a founder and coordinating committee member of Build Programs, Not Jails, an anti-jail campaign in opposition to jail construction in Champaign from 2012 until 2018. He is the author of five books, including Understanding E-Carceration *and the award-winning* Understanding Mass Incarceration *(both from the New Press). He has also written numerous articles on mass incarceration and the history of southern Africa and won a Soros Justice Fellowship in 2017.*

Judah Schept: Thank you for speaking with me, James. We first met in 2011 when you reached out to a few of us who had been involved in a campaign against jail expansion in Bloomington, Indiana. At that time, your community of Champaign-Urbana was in the middle of its own, similar fight. To start us off, could you start by talking about the campaign against the jail and the work of your group in particular?

James Kilgore: Well, let me put this in a personal context to begin. I paroled from prison to Champaign, Illinois, in 2009. And I decided that I wanted to lay low while I was on parole, because I had a high-profile case. And the first thing I did as a kind of political engagement was to organize two reading groups of *The New Jim Crow*, which was hot off the press at the time. Those reading groups probably had altogether about twenty-five people, where we went through the book a chapter a week pretty meticulously. I think that study group galvanized the political consciousness of a lot of people in the community, and particularly around the connection between mass incarceration and racism. Not long after that, the county sheriff and the state's attorney attended a workshop in Colorado, which they described in an email that we FOIA'd as a "How to Build a Jail" workshop. They acted on the mandate of that workshop and tried to bring forward a proposal to build a jail. Champaign County had two jails at the time: one downtown, which was built in 1980 and which held a hundred and thirty-one people at that time, and another one, which is kind of on the periphery of Urbana, which held one hundred eighty-two people and was built in 1996. The sheriff wanted to close the downtown jail, because it was a rat hole, and spend something in the neighborhood of twenty million dollars to extend, modify, and revamp the satellite jail that was in the suburbs. So, at a personal level, I felt like, wow, you've given my life a purpose here. I've been paroled after having lived eighteen years in southern Africa and then spent six and a half years in prisons. And then I moved to this almost all-white college town and I'm like a stranger in a strange land. I got no way to engage with what's going on here and I don't really relate to the folks. And then the sheriff comes along with this proposal, and I say, "Damn, this is a good moment to become active!"

Judah: Did the sheriff have support? And was there an existing organization to work with, or did you help to develop one that could focus on the jail fight?

James: We had one county board member at the time, Carol Ammons, who has since become the state representative, who stood up at county board meetings and said, "You're not building this jail, we don't need a jail. All it is for is locking up Black people in this county. We need mental health. We need reentry programs, we need a whole range of services, but we don't need to add on to the jail." I think there were twenty-two people on the county board at the time. If they had taken a straw vote, right at that moment, it probably would have been something like twenty-one to one, with Carol the lone vote in opposition. Everybody else [on the board and in criminal justice positions] bought the idea that the old jail was terrible, and the satellite jail did not have enough space. Plus the sheriff was pushing a security line, that the guards weren't safe and all that. In their heart of hearts I think the county board and the sheriff were also into legacy. They wanted to build a shiny new jail so they could claim that as their contribution to the county.

Carol, myself, and a couple of other people, Chris Evans and Jerehme Bamberger, who at the time were part of what was called Champaign Urbana Citizens for Peace and Justice (CUCPJ) formed a subcommittee, which would eventually become Build Programs Not Jails (BPNJ). We started doing research on the jail and speaking at the county board meetings. We had some offline conversations with other county board members. Eventually, we played an obstructionist game. We said, "Well, you can't spend twenty million dollars in Champaign County without having a study. You've got to have somebody do some research on this and more precisely tell us what's needed." We convinced some of the more fence-sitting Democrats to agree to a study. We then went through a whole process of hiring a consultant. We tried to find a consultant who was legitimate, who might fit our perspective on this. And we found Alan Kalmanoff, God rest his soul, who had been doing this work for years. He came with one fatal flaw—he was from Berkeley, California. We figured that as soon as he landed here, they would see that and throw him out. But in the final shortlist of candidates, there were three consultants, and the other two both had strong ties to jail construction companies. They had a whole history that we could use to show that they were basically just stooges for the jail builders. But Kalmanoff said, "I don't work with construction companies. I will not, in any way, sign any kind of deal or make any kind of connection with a construction company." And the county board members liked that. Then the final maneuver we made was to get the vote on the consultant to be a secret ballot. Because if it had been a roll call or "raise your hand" ballot, all of the Republicans would have had to vote for one of these other two people. But since it was a secret ballot, Kalmanoff won.

Kalmanoff was just one of those people who could sit down and talk with anybody. He would sit down with the state's attorney and talk for two hours with her over lunch, just so he had talked to people all over the county. He also met with our organization. That created a big debate and discussion that provided extra space for us to raise the complexities of building a jail and for us to do our own research. We were the first ones to ever really research the population. What we found was in a county that's thirteen percent Black, that the jail population fluctuated between fifty and seventy percent Black. Another big push for the consultants [and for a new jail] was that the women [supposedly] needed a separate jail. [Based on our research we were able to say] "Well, there are very few women in this jail, at times there's only five or six of them." The county board members had no idea about this. So we created a whole debate and discussion, which then reverberated sort of in the social justice community and to some extent in the Black community.

Toward the end of 2013, Kalmanoff released his report, which recommended a bunch of changes. He agreed we needed some upgrades to the jail. But he also said that we needed mental health facilities, we needed what he called a "sobering center," and a whole range of facilities that didn't exist. We then pushed for the formation of a Community Justice Task Force, and we got a whole range of people involved. So Carol ended up chairing that Community Justice Task Force. We got lawyers, a state's attorney, myself, and a couple of other anti-jail advocates from the university. We produced a long report that basically called for ten recommendations, like having mental health facilities, setting up a pretrial services department, reducing bail, a whole range of funds, basically, which together created a pretty powerful, reformist agenda. One of the recommendations was that we needed a Racial Justice Task Force to investigate why we had so many Black people in the jail.

When it came time for the 2014 budget, at the end of 2013, we got the county board to basically refuse to allocate any funding to the jail. We wanted them to fund reentry and pretrial services. We had drafted a kind of RFP for the reentry proposal. Our main premise was that we wanted formerly incarcerated people to be driving that reentry program. The county board wasn't gonna have any of that. They funded a really bogus reentry program, run by some local nonprofit, which does absolutely nothing for anybody. The board also gave money to form pretrial services. And the state's attorney, the sheriff, and the chief judge *gave the money back* because they said we didn't need a pretrial services program. So, I mean, we won, but we weren't able to really get a lot of the changes going. But basically, we had pushed the jail out the way. That's Round One. It was early 2014. We had a celebration that we'd won this victory and we kind of were patting ourselves on the back. And then came Round Two.

Judah: What happened? How did Round Two differ from the first iteration of the fight?

James: This is what gave me the notion of carceral humanism.

After about three or four months, the sheriff came back with a different architect and a thirty-two-million-dollar plan. He started using the language of, "We want to make things better for the inmates—we have to have better mental health services, we have to have better visiting, we have to make sure that things are livable for these people so that they're not being excessively punished." He completely changed his messaging and cast us as being the villains who wanted to keep these poor folks in these horrible jail cells, rather than give them a nice, soft bed to sleep on, and a big gymnasium to play basketball. So we then had to back up and reframe how we approached this.

Every time the sheriff raised the proposal, the county board members who were sitting on the fence would say, "Oh yeah, that makes sense—we have to listen to the sheriff." They continually fall for the bullshit. Then we would need to go back to them and say, "Well, hang on. Let's talk about this. You know, do we really need the jail? For how many?" You have to take them back and remind them, "We just had two years of struggle over this, and you forgot it all? Remember how many Black people we got in this jail? Remember the fact that we got no mental health facilities? Remember the fact that we have no sobering center, substance use treatment, et cetera?" The jail is the catch-all for all these people that have all these issues and they're being criminalized, because the jail is all we've got to handle them. We even had a lot of the Urbana police stepping up and saying, "We don't want to pick up people with mental health issues, we're picking up the same guys six times in a month, and we take them out to jail, and they walk out the next morning. How is this doing any good?" So, we began to get some curious allies.

A couple of things then happened. We agitated and stalled around the second proposal. The county board knew that they didn't have the money to build. They owed a lot of debt. So until they paid off some of those bonds on previous jail construction and other issues, they weren't going to have money to build this jail. They also had an ADA inspection. The jail was not up to date on ADA standards and were called on the carpet by ADA inspectors and being forced to give a timeline as to when they're going to deal with that. We also were entering a different political moment here. We have what's the beginning of a very active but short-lived Black Lives Matter chapter. One of the persons who actually founded the BLM chapter, Evelyn Reynolds, came from Build Programs Not Jails.

So, all of a sudden, Black Lives Matter was able to mobilize twenty, thirty people, mostly from on campus, around this issue. Our pressure at that point—we're talking about late 2015, early 2016—was to get the county to form a Racial Justice Task Force. We had a very dramatic meeting, unlike any meeting I've ever seen in Champaign County, where Black Lives Matter came in numbers. They, along with some allies, really shouted down the county board. They created a climate where we could see that the board members were scared. They were actually afraid. I feel that they were afraid that they weren't going to be able to physically leave the room. I mean, of course, that's not what came about. But that's the feeling that I got from them. And then I've never seen that level of conflict in an official meeting in small town USA. People were standing up and singing and chanting and holding placards and doing all kinds of stuff to kind of upset the general business of the county board. The county board members were just in a state of shock. They ended up by the end of the meeting voting to put this Racial Justice Task Force in place, but also took out a couple of clauses that were put there by BLM regarding Black leadership. So BLM members weren't pleased with the outcome. Personally, I thought it was better than we probably ever expected to get. There was more activist and more Black presence on that task force than I've probably seen in anything in the recent history of the county. They did a pretty reasonable job of doing research, of having people come and give testimony, and produced a report with a set of recommendations that were pretty strong and powerful.

At the same time as this was going on, we also had a series of deaths in the jail. In the course of six months, we had three Black people who died in the jail. Two of them had something to do with drugs and going through withdrawal. One person had an asthma attack. He was in jail after being arrested for driving with a suspended license, and he died in a jail cell of an asthma attack. This also created a whole big contradictory stir, because on the one hand people were saying, "You people running this jail are horrific and racist," but at the same time you had people wanting to improve the conditions at the jail, who were trying to use [the deaths in custody] to say, "You see, we need better conditions."

In 2016, we got a new county administrator. He sparked a new round of desires to build a jail. He proposed a point-two-five percent public facility sales tax to fund the demolition of the downtown jail and to build the addition onto the satellite jail. At the same time, there was a battle going on over the county nursing home, which also wanted to propose a property tax because they weren't financially surviving. There wound up being a referendum on the 2016 November ballot for a point twenty-five percent sales tax for public facilities, with sixty percent of that going to law-enforcement facilities. The estimate was that it would generate like fifty million dollars over twelve years.

So this is one of the great contradictory moments in my political history. I remember the night of that election on the sales tax referendum, a bunch of us from Build Programs Not Jails went out to the county administration building to watch the count as it came in. We were kicking their asses. But we're all sitting there on our phones going, "What the fuck is happening in the national election?" By the end of the night, we had slaughtered them on the sales tax, but Trump had won the presidency.

Judah: What kind of coalition constituted the opposition to the sales tax referendum to generate that kind of victory?

James: I'm thinking that we got support from the unions on that. I'm sure we got support from the NAACP. On this campus [University of Illinois-Champaign Urbana] we have a really powerful graduate students' organization. They've got a very broad political consciousness and have supported everything BPNJ ever did. We did have a broad coalition. There's two layers of opposition to the jail in this county. There's the liberal opposition, that doesn't like jail building. Then there's the conservative opposition that doesn't want to spend a penny on "these fucking criminals." This is a county where sixty percent of the people live in Champaign-Urbana. But forty percent of the population lives in these small, mostly all-white farm towns. And, you know, those are Republicans. But they don't want to spend money on "criminals." They never showed up.

Judah: With the defeat of the sales tax, was that essentially the nail in the coffin of building out this new addition?

James: Oh, no.

Judah: There is a Part Three?

James: Unfortunately, there's a Part Three. And the Part Three is the bad part.

In March 2017 we called for a meeting to organize some kind of massive pushback against Trump. We had about two hundred people come out for this. People were just so angry and ready to do something. We weren't too sure what. I feel like we missed the moment there. I think we could have consolidated something and probably magnified both the population and the power of our political organization. But we kind of stalled and weren't sure how to move forward. It was one of those moments where you've got momentum, and you gotta either jump on it or it goes away. From there, the jail kind of faded into the woodwork. The county board basically realized there was no way they were going to ever raise the money to build this jail. They tried a referendum that didn't work. They didn't have enough money in their budget to both keep paying their bills and set aside twenty million dollars for a new jail. In 2019, before the pandemic, the architects came back with one more round. But it was half baked, because everybody knew that they just didn't have the money for it. So it just kind of faded away and Build Programs Not Jails had essentially disappeared by then as well.

Then came the ARPA (American Rescue Plan Act) funds following the onset of the pandemic. The Democrats by this time had a fourteen-to-eight majority on the county board. Almost all of them had declared upon election that they would not spend the money on a jail. But you know how that goes. The sheriff came and started singing this sad song about "we don't have enough deputies, we need better visiting, the downtown jail is falling apart, it will cost us X amount of dollars to replace all the locks, and the only solution we have now is to start sending people out of the county, which is very expensive." Basically, the liberals started to melt. Then comes forty-one million dollars to the county through ARPA funds. By this time, my political work in the county was focused on reentry. We were building out the First Followers organization and trying to pull together a coalition to get some of that ARPA money for the issue of community violence. Because, you know, there's a lot of deaths in Champaign County from gun violence, and probably ninety-five percent were young Black men. It took a lot of pressure from us and other people to put this onto the agenda of the County Board and the city councils, who also got ARPA money.

We were negotiating with Democrats on the county board to get money for community violence prevention, but at the same time, they were also negotiating with the sheriff. So we were in the position of saying, "well, we don't really want to see money going to the jail. But our main priority is to get money for the community violence prevention work." Basically political horse trading. They ended up giving five million dollars of ARPA money to the jail and agreed that they could afford to grab a bond for another twenty million. They've already closed the downtown jail. In 2023 they're going to flesh out all the plans for the new jail and in 2024 they'll do construction. One of the things that's happened in the middle of this is that the jail population has just escalated beyond previous levels. The main reason this has happened is because in the county you've got a triumvirate of decision makers in law enforcement: the state's attorney, the chief judge, and the sheriff. They come together and map out what needs to happen. The sheriff wants more jail. The state's attorney always wants more law enforcement. Apparently, from what we understand, she's stopped making attractive plea-bargain offers. So people stay in jail, because they're not going to take these shit deals that she's offering. That grows the jail population. The last time I checked, which was a couple of weeks ago, the jail population was up over three hundred. During our work as BPNJ, we had the jail population down to like one hundred forty, one hundred fifty.

Judah: What's the anticipated size for new jail construction? How many beds are they talking about? How much would it expand capacity?

James: It's not much. I think it's somewhere around two hundred thirty or two hundred forty. Whereas before the downtown jail and the satellite jails together were three hundred thirteen. That's also part of how they're selling this: "Oh, it's no net new beds." That's one of their favorite lines, "no net new beds."

But we've had times when that downtown jail had, like, ten people. I mean, the downtown jail is a shithole. I mean, it should be torn down. I went on a tour of the downtown jail. Everybody else that was on the tour was just like, "Oh my God, oh my God." I'm kind of sitting there going, "Huh. Y'all don't know much about jails and prisons, you know?" Yeah, it's bad. But what do you think [Illinois maximum security prisons] Stateville or Pontiac looks like inside? What do you think these other county jails in southern Illinois look like? I mean, you think this is so unusual? But they don't know.

Judah: Would you talk more about Build Programs Not Jails as an organization?

James: When BPNJ became a separate organization from Champaign Urbana Citizens for Peace and Justice, we started out as a small group, but sometimes we got to the point where we'd have twenty or thirty people at our meetings. So we decided we would have a steering committee, which would be three or four people, and the steering committee would meet between meetings, take any decisions that needed to be taken between meetings, and would then create the agenda for the next meeting and would rotate the facilitation. I think that structure worked quite well. That structure enabled us to do the kinds of campaign work that we did. We went out into different neighborhoods and did surveys door-to-door, asking people, "If you had twenty million dollars to spend, what would you do with it?" We interviewed one hundred twenty-seven people total. I think seven people said they would build a jail or use it for policing. Everybody else had housing, streetlights, whatever. One person said he'd spend it on Chuck E. Cheese. But, there was no sentiment for that jail. We, of course, used that survey then as a way to discuss the jail.

We went to the farmers' market every Saturday and got people to sign petitions against jail construction. We mobilized people from all over the country to write letters and postcards. Michelle Alexander wrote a letter to our county board chair and cc'd all the county board members. We had people from California, from New York, we had people from all over the place. I think you all (members of Decarcerate Monroe County, in Indiana) probably wrote some stuff, too, because I remember you came and spoke at a public forum that we had in the city council chambers. The county board chair at one of the meetings held up this stack of like two hundred fifty postcards from different people saying that they didn't want money spent on the jail. All of these approaches were about getting people mobilized and making the county board members see that we had some support and that maybe it was going to create some problems for them if they just decided to go and spend twenty million dollars of the county's money. We mobilized people on the county board. We developed strategic plans. Just a whole range of things that required more of a sustained structure than simply sending out an email on Monday night saying, "Can everybody come to the county board meeting on Thursday?" All that kind of stuff, I think, made a difference in terms of our effectiveness. Build Programs Not Jails was quite an effective organization for, like, five or six years.

Judah: Can you expand on that? What made BPNJ's efforts effective and what lessons do you think such experiences might offer to other organizers struggling against jail expansion?

James: Broadly speaking, I think our campaign was successful, even though in the end we were defeated. We need to examine how we were able to succeed and also look at some of the weaknesses of our campaign as we move along.

1. The first key to our campaign was that from the start we maintained an ideological opposition to building jail cells. We had to fight off liberals, we had to fight off some church people who felt sorry for the "poor inmates," but we had to fight off and hold that line. It wasn't always easy. There were times when we would get professors from the university

saying, "We need mental health facilities in these jails, these people are human beings too." All that kind of stuff. But we had to be able to mount a political argument against that that wasn't just, "Fuck you, we're not building a jail."

2. We became the experts on that jail. We knew more about that jail and that system than anybody. So *we* had to teach *them*. We had to teach them what was going on in their jail and what were the options for doing something other than jail building. That was really critical. Ruthie [Wilson Gilmore] likes to say, "If you're an activist, you have got to be a nerd." Yeah, you've got to be a nerd. You've got to do FOIA requests. You've got to research, to know more than they do.

3. You've got to build relationships with the decision makers and be able to engage with the existing system. You don't have to like them. But you've got to be able to have a conversation. You can't just attack them as "you fucking fascist, blah, blah." You've got to be able to have conversations with them. A lot of activists don't get that—"that's the enemy." Well, yeah, they're the enemy. But you cannot change the criminal legal system without engaging with the system. If you're dealing with jails and prisons, you can't go build a jail over here and say, "Well, this is the 'people's jail'." Now, you *can* do that with some things, like a therapy program or mutual aid. You can build alternative systems and show what a new world would look like. But if you're trying to fight a jail build, or if you're trying to get people out of jail, you have to engage the system that they're in.

4. You have to have a structure to your campaign. You have to have decision-making structures. You have to have regular meetings, minutes, follow-ups, structured campaigns, deadlines, all those things that make a structured organization. It doesn't have to be centralized. You don't necessarily need

a CEO or whatever. I mean, I'm personally not opposed to having a director or a campaign captain or whatever. But you have to have some leadership. You can't just have decision-making by consensus all the time. We mostly operated with consensus. We could get to consensus through debate and discussion, but there's times when there is no consensus, and then you've got to have a way to make a decision. But through it all we had a core of people who were consistent leadership: Kristina Khan, Rohn Koester, Dottie Vura-Weis, Niloofar Shambayati were key along the way.

5. Lastly, I'd say that we never really figured out how to engage with the Black community around this issue. I mean, we leafletted, we talked to people, we had public meetings. Black people came but we weren't able to get them as part of the campaign. I don't think that's an unusual experience in majority-white spaces where people try to organize but don't have any experience of building alliances with other populations. In the end it's a fatal flaw. Because although I think we impacted the consciousness of the Black population here, at the same time, now that we have gun violence and so forth, there's a significant element in the Black population that wants a policing solution. So we had a battle around license-plate readers, we've had a battle around shot spotters, battles around cameras. Because we didn't really build out the narrative of mass incarceration and abolition, we weren't able to attract a significant number of people from the Black population. Now, some of that is also due to less of a tradition of community organizing in the Black population here. It's the NAACP, which is small and not very powerful. And it's churches, who are not really activists. Not every place is Jackson, Mississippi. Although there's a visceral opposition to policing and jails, at the same time, when your children start getting killed, that social justice committee at the university isn't going to really do anything. I think we probably

should have made more of an effort to engage people that have been in the jail and engage their families. It's not easy. I think these are questions that need some reflection. A place like Chicago, with a massive Black population and a long history of organizing, it's a different terrain. I'm not saying it's easier, but it's different. And people want to organize Champaign and turn it into Chicago overnight. Probably not going to happen.

Judah: I think this is precisely why these kinds of stories are so crucial, because we just don't have that many of them about places like Champaign-Urbana. The dynamics are different, the politics are different, local economic history is different, the racial politics are different. And yet, there's still fights around building new jails or putting more cops on the street. We need to understand these kinds of campaigns, the successes, the missteps, in their specific contexts in order to build out a more complete sense of the geography of mass incarceration.

James: One of the things that I always struggle with in the debates and discussion is how little attention people pay to organization. For me, and for abolitionists, this is like, "Okay, here is what we have imagined. What kind of organization do we need to get there, that's going to get us to that vision, and is going to be able to fight the people that are going to try to stop us from getting there at the same time?" Because we can't imagine a new reality without having quite a nasty fight for it. Restorative circles are useful, but they're not going to deal with engaging the state, engaging law enforcement, engaging the prison industrial complex, right? What does that organization look like?

3

County Jails and the
Immigrant Dragnet

Silky Shah

"Simply, without healthy partnerships between the federal, state, and local governments, DHS cannot accomplish this mission as effectively as it does through IGSAs. Further, local governments would not have the opportunity to be better trained and equipped by being involved in the bigger picture of securing our homeland. We are pleased to work alongside the men and women of DHS to accomplish what none can alone."
　　　　—Todd Entrekin, sheriff of Etowah County, Alabama[1]

In the summer of 2018, not long after Trump enacted a zero-tolerance policy for families arriving at the southern border, Knox County, Tennessee, experienced a 300 percent rise in the number of immigrants detained at its county jail.[2] Knox County had been increasing its partnership with Immigration and Customs Enforcement (ICE) since the previous year when it entered into a 287(g) agreement that gave local police the

---

1 *Border Security and Enforcement: Department of Homeland Security's Cooperation with State and Local Law Enforcement Stakeholders: Hearing Before the Subcommittee on Border and Maritime Security of the Committee on Homeland Security*, House of Representatives, 112th Cong., 1st Session (May 3, 2011).

2 Tyler Whetstone, "Knox County ICE Detainees Spike after Ex-Sheriff Signs New Agreement," *Knoxville News Sentinel*, September 9, 2018, knoxnews.com.

ability to act as immigration enforcers. Yet, while the 287(g) agreement gave the county more latitude to target immigrants for deportation, the number of people in ICE custody at the jail skyrocketed only after the county signed an intergovernmental service agreement (IGSA) with ICE to detain immigrants. Knox County then became a hub for immigration detention in Tennessee, thanks to this IGSA agreement. ICE currently pays the county eighty-three dollars a day 'per bed occupied,' and immigrants from across the state are detained in the jail, often for seventy-two hours, before they are transferred to larger detention centers in Louisiana while they await a hearing on their immigration case or deportation.[3]

Knox County's arrangement with ICE is far from unique. The mass detention of immigrants is one component of the larger carceral landscape in the US, and county jails are the bedrock of the detention system. While much of the narrative on immigrant incarceration singles out the role of private prisons, a parasitic industry that has benefited from the expanding deportation machine, local governments and sheriff's departments are key players in ICE's agenda to arrest, detain, and deport as many immigrants as possible. Combined, ICE and the United States Marshals Service (USMS) have upward of 1,200 intergovernmental agreements with counties across the country, and in recent years about 75 percent of ICE capacity involved these types of agreements.[4] This phenomenon has created a symbiotic relationship between the federal government and local counties, in which ICE and USMS outsource their detention operations

---

3 Megan Conley and Nathan Hilbert, "Knox County's 287(g) Program and Detention Bed Contract," Allies of Knoxville's Immigrant Neighbors, September 25, 2020, weareakin.wordpress.com.

4 Jesse Franzblau, "Cut the Contracts: It's Time to End ICE's Corrupt Detention Management System," policy brief, National Immigrant Justice Center, March 16, 2021, immigrantjustice.org; Seth Freed Wessler, "Inside the US Marshals' Secretive, Deadly Detention Empire," *Mother Jones*, November/December 2019, motherjones.com.

to meet the ebb and flow of their priorities, while not having to manage their own facilities that are often more expensive to maintain. County governments, meanwhile, have become dependent on these lucrative federal agreements, and some sheriffs will vie for contracts and expand jails to create more bedspace to generate revenue for their dwindling municipal budgets or, in some instances, to pocket the money outright.[5]

A recent study has revealed that immigrants are 2.3 times more likely to be arrested in counties with detention capacity of more than fifty people. In counties with detention capacity of more than 850 the likelihood of arrest went up by a factor of 6.4.[6] The Knox County example illuminates the role that ICE collaboration with county jails and local police plays in the immigrant dragnet. Many immigrant rights advocates have raised concerns about ending contracts between ICE and local jails in fear that immigrants will be transferred far away from family and counsel. But these arguments fail to consider that the mere existence of detention bed space in a county or region increases the likelihood that someone will be arrested because of their immigration status. Ending local contracts with ICE is essential to disrupting this dragnet.

During the Obama era, as deportations surged, immigrant justice organizers and advocates targeted sheriffs and county agreements to protect immigrant communities from ICE's reach. Initially, tactics involved ending collaborations between local law enforcement and ICE, but in recent years, organizers have also focused on ending ICE contracts with county jails through local- and state-level campaigns. Despite growing opposition to

---

5 Connor Sheets, "Etowah Sheriff Pockets $750k in Jail Food Funds, Buys $740k Beach House," *Birmingham Real-Time News*, March 13, 2018, al.com.

6 Gabriela Viera, *If You Build It, ICE Will Fill It: The Link Between Detention Capacity and ICE Arrests* (Detention Watch Network, Immigrant Legal Resource Center, Ceres Policy Research, September 29, 2022), ilrc.org.

these contracts, many local officials have resisted ending ICE collaboration due to the potential loss in revenue and jobs. In some instances, members of Congress have intervened to keep federal contracts in place.

However, as immigrant justice activists have increasingly fought detention expansion and exposed ICE misconduct and abuse, more states have opted to eliminate IGSAs with the federal agencies. While ending these contracts is an important tactic to disrupt the dragnet, in every instance where ICE is forced out, the county jail previously used for immigration detention has remained open, leaving sheriffs and county officials looking for other ways to supplement revenue lost from canceled contracts and per diem payments. In many cases underlying USMS contracts with jail operators remain in place, which means people arrested for federal crimes, including immigrants targeted by the federal government for prosecution, are still locked up in these jails, with local sheriff's departments still receiving per diem payments from USMS. Since 2005, immigration crimes, specifically for unauthorized entry and reentry, have become one of the most prosecuted federal crimes.[7] By better understanding the relationship between counties and the federal government and the various tactics used by organizers in recent years, we can determine the best way to push not just for the end to ICE detention, but to stop jail expansion more broadly.

The Proliferation of Intergovernmental Service Agreements

The modern immigration detention system began to take shape in the early 1980s when the convergence of Cold War era anti-immigrant policy and the US prison boom resulted in the Immigration Naturalization Service (INS) becoming a mass

---

7 John Gramlich, "Far More Immigration Cases Are Being Prosecuted Criminally under Trump Administration," Pew Research Center, September 27, 2019, pewresearch.org.

jailer. Since then, when detention was a rare practice, the system has grown exponentially, and by 2019, before the onset of the COVID-19 pandemic, some 400,000 immigrants were detained annually. Other than the five detention centers the federal government owns and operates in Arizona, Florida, New York, and Texas, where there are two, all ICE detention is subcontracted out to county jails and private prison corporations. The only instances in which ICE has direct contracts with private prison companies, which require a lengthy and public competitive bidding process, are contract detention facilities. However, in recent years ICE has circumvented this process by issuing "sole source" awards, which remove competitive bidding and move more quickly to secure or renew contracts with private companies.[8] The process for entering intergovernmental service agreements (IGSAs) where ICE contracts with counties to rent out bed space at local jails is even more opaque. Sometimes ICE sends out a statement of objectives to sheriffs or county officials to see who bites, or ICE will reach out directly to see if there is space available. In addition to IGSAs, ICE often adds riders to existing US Marshals Service contracts with local jails in order to use them for immigration detention.[9]

Most ICE contracts are intergovernmental service agreements that afford little transparency. In some cases, these contracts entail counties playing intermediaries between the federal government and private prison companies. One example of this involved the 2014 opening of the South Texas Family Detention Center (Dilley) in Dilley, Texas. In 2009, President Barack Obama's first year in office, ICE ended the practice of family detention at the T. Don Hutto facility, a private immigration detention center in Taylor, Texas, thereby signaling the

8 "Government Contracts and Immigration Detention Services," Immigrant Legal Resource Center, October 24, 2019, ilrc.org.

9 Jack Norton and Jacob Kang-Brown, "If You Build It: How the Federal Government Fuels Rural Jail Expansion," *In Our Backyards Stories*, January 10, 2020, vera.org.

administration's reluctance to detain children. But in 2014, with an increase in families arriving at the border, the Obama administration retreated from its earlier position and opened two new family detention centers, arguing that it was a necessary policy to deter migration. Dilley, a 2,400-bed Corrections Corporation of America–operated (now CoreCivic) facility located between San Antonio and Laredo in south Texas, was built in a matter of weeks, which was only possible because of the IGSA model. To move quickly, ICE added a rider to an existing IGSA contract with the City of Eloy in Arizona, located 900 miles from Dilley. Eloy has been contracting for years as a middleman between ICE and CCA and receives annual fees of $438,000. However, in 2018, an eighteen-month-old toddler, Mariee, died after being detained at Dilley, and when the mother sued the City of Eloy for $40 million, Eloy removed the contract rider to evade liability.[10] In the aftermath of this news, local organizers in Texas hoped they might be able to shut down Dilley and block a new contract. Yet, after inquiring about the contract negotiations they discovered that ICE had signed an IGSA with the City of Dilley the day the news broke about Eloy, exposing how quickly IGSA contracts can be put into place.

The story of Dilley's expansion is just one example of how IGSAs have been used as a tool to expand immigration detention without transparency or opportunity for public comment. This is exactly why the IGSA has been the contract of choice for the federal government since the early eighties when the federal jail population began to grow. While IGSAs involving private prisons may not be as lucrative for the county, many local officials see these arrangements as job creators and a potential source of revenue. Private prison companies will often pay counties fees for being the intermediary, including, for example, a payment of one dollar a day per person detained,

---

10 Paul Ingram, "Sued for $40M in Toddler's Death, Eloy Cancels 'Middleman' Deal with ICE Detention Center in Texas," *Tucson Sentinel*, September 26, 2018, tucsonsentinel.com.

further incentivizing the relationship.[11] Some fourteen private detention centers involve these types of arrangements, where the county contracts with the federal government and also the private prison company for immigration detention. But public county jails have always played an important role in the deportation pipeline. Over 130 of the 200 ICE detention centers involve IGSAs between the federal government and county jails, not private prisons.

A Symbiotic Relationship

In 1997, shortly after Congress passed two draconian immigration bills that greatly expanded the scope of who could be detained and deported, the Etowah County Jail in Alabama started detaining immigrants for INS. After Congress established the Department of Homeland Security (DHS) in 2002, the budget for immigration enforcement tripled from less than $4 billion to $12.5 billion by 2006.[12] During this period, the newly created ICE bankrolled an expansion of Etowah, paying $8.4 million of the $13.5 million project to increase capacity and create a separate women's unit.[13]

The Etowah County Jail, in northeastern Alabama, is one of the most notorious jails ever used for immigration detention. Despite the influx of funds for expansion, the county failed to build any sort of outdoor recreation, which meant people

---

11 Angilee Shah, "An Immigration Detention Center in Farmville Built for over 700 People Now Has 11—and Activists Say It's Time to Shut It Down," *Charlottesville Tomorrow*, May 9, 2022, cvilletomorrow.org.

12 Muzzaffer Chisti and Jessica Bolter, "Two Decades after 9/11, National Security Focus Still Dominates U.S. Immigration System," Migration Policy Institute, September 22, 2021, migrationpolicy.org.

13 Donna Thornton, "Key Dates in the ICE–Etowah County Detention Center Partnership," *Gadsden Times*, March 25, 2022, gadsdentimes.com.

incarcerated at the jail never set foot outside. While this would be considered inhumane for any amount of time, Etowah often incarcerated immigrants who were appealing their deportation cases, which meant some individuals would spend months or years in the jail without access to sunlight and fresh air. An Office of Detention Oversight (part of ICE) inspection of the facility in 2012 revealed the sham nature of ICE oversight, stating that "the designated outdoor recreation facilities were found to be enclosed areas with secure openings that allow natural lighting and air circulation." In other words, a room with a window was sufficient for outdoor recreation.[14]

Under the Obama administration, ICE attempted to reform the detention system after facing growing outrage over conditions and deaths in detention, but it also faced challenges from some sheriff's departments and elected officials. ICE prioritized moving away from the vast network of county jail contracts to large immigrant-only private prisons closer to metropolitan cities with more access to family and counsel. In December 2010, as part of this plan, ICE announced that it would no longer use Etowah, due to its distance from immigrant communities, but Etowah sheriff Todd Entrekin organized Republican members of Congress to protect the contract and keep revenue from ICE flowing to the county. He reached out to Alabama's Republican delegation in Congress and pointed out to them that the IGSA brought in more than $5 million a year in revenue, and that the county would lose 49 jobs if the contract ended. The county was also paying a $3 million debt from the previous jail expansion. Entrekin told *The Gadsden Times* that "without the ICE contract, Etowah County will not be able to meet these obligations." Representatives Robert Aderholt and Mike Rogers, along with Alabama's senators, Richard Shelby and Jeff Sessions, sent emails and met with ICE to keep the contract in

---

14 *Lives in Peril: How Ineffective Inspections Make ICE Complicit in Detention Abuse* (Detention Watch Network and National Immigrant Justice Center, October 2015), detentionwatchnetwork.org.

place.[15] Since Aderholt had recently become chairman of the House Appropriations Subcommittee on Homeland Security, he had unique power over ICE's budget. At the time, ICE was in regular negotiations with Congress over an arbitrary quota put in place in Obama's first year in office that required ICE maintain a certain number of beds for detention. DHS argued that maintaining capacity while trying to improve conditions would require additional resources. Aderholt leveraged his position on the subcommittee to threaten ICE's funding, and the agency relented. In an email to ICE staff, Gary Mead, ICE's executive associate director for Enforcement and Removal Operations (ERO), wrote, "I met with Aderholt's personal staff … I do not believe we will be allowed to leave Etowah without serious repercussions against our budget. I have a meeting tomorrow with ERO folks to figure out if there is a reasonable way to make some use of Etowah long term. Discretion may be the better part of valor here."[16] The sheriff and Alabama Republicans in Congress had succeeded, and Etowah remained available to ICE.

Etowah is not the only instance where the federal government bankrolled local jail expansion to meet its detention needs. In the early 2000s when INS was part of the Department of Justice, the Office of the Federal Detention Trustee was tasked with developing "a comprehensive National Detention Strategy to address the nation's increasing detention needs."[17] The goal: to ensure bedspace was readily available for INS, USMS, and the Federal Bureau of Prisons, in both public and private facilities. The office eventually merged into USMS in 2012, but in the

15 Lisa Riordan Seville and Hannah Rappleye, "When Feds Fought to Shutter Immigration Jail, Politics Intervened," nbcnews.com, August 22, 2012.
16 Ibid.
17 US Department of Justice, Office of the Attorney General, *The Accomplishments of the U.S. Department of Justice, 2001–2009*, justice. gov.

decade or so it existed the impact was significant. ICE capacity during that time went from 20,429 average daily population in 2001 to 34,260 in 2012.[18] During the Trump years that number reached its height with an average daily population of 50,165 in 2019.[19]

As the detention system has expanded, sheriffs across the country have increasingly seen IGSA contracts as a potential source of revenue. ICE pays on average $133 a day to detain immigrants, though county jails often receive lower per diems than private prisons.[20] For years, ICE has been trying to secure more space for immigration detention in the Midwest. In response, several sheriffs have not only offered existing bed-space but have proposed to expand their county jails to meet ICE's demand. In 2018, Calhoun County, Michigan, which already had a 250-bed contract with ICE bringing in about $4 million a year in revenue, considered a 300-bed expansion as precursor to a bigger ICE contract. Other counties in the Midwest followed suit, and Sherburne County, Minnesota, and Kankakee County, Illinois, proposed expansions of their jails to meet ICE's needs.[21] Since then, detention numbers have retreated due to the COVID-19 pandemic, but that hasn't stopped some counties from pursuing expansion. In 2022, after Illinois passed state legislation banning IGSAs, officials in Clay County, Indiana, saw an opportunity to secure additional per

18 J. Rachel Reyes, "Immigration Detention: Recent Trends and Scholarship," Center for Migration Studies, March 26, 2018, cmsny.org.

19 US Immigration and Customs Enforcement, Enforcement and Removal Operations, *U.S. Immigration and Customs Enforcement Fiscal Year 2019 Enforcement and Removal Operations Report* (2019), ice.gov.

20 US Department of Homeland Security, Immigration and Customs Enforcement, "Fiscal Year 2018, Congressional Justification" (2018), dhs.gov.

21 Brad Devereaux, "Sheriff Runs $6M Jail 'Boarding Business' That Holds ICE Detainees," *Michigan Live*, May, 4, 2018, mlive.com; Adam Geller, "Michigan County Pitches for Immigration Detention Site," *Detroit News*, May 11, 2018, detroitnews.com.

diems from ICE and are currently considering a $25 million expansion of their current jail to add 265 beds.[22]

Local Campaigns, National Impact

After twenty-four years of detaining immigrants at Etowah County Jail, DHS finally ended its use on April 30, 2022. Much had changed since 2011, when ICE reversed course on its plan to phase out use of the jail. Organizers, advocates, lawyers, and people detained came together to launch the Shut Down Etowah campaign in 2015 to expose the harm of the jail, free people, and end ICE detention at Etowah. As more campaigns like this started popping up across the country after Trump's election, preventing and ending IGSAs became a key strategy in the struggle against the federal government's detention agenda. In 2018, at the height of Trump's expansion spree, Detention Watch Network launched the Communities Not Cages campaign to support local efforts against detention, and to connect organizers across the country to learn from one another's fights. Local organizers and advocates have employed a range of tactics to end IGSAs: meeting with county and state officials; participating in public comment during hearings; staging community educational events; organizing actions, sometimes including civil disobedience; supporting organizing inside jails; litigating conditions; engaging local media; and organizing campaigns around individual cases to free people from detention. Through these efforts, more immigrant rights organizations began to support the idea of detention abolition, as did some elected officials.

The results have been encouraging. Thanks to a combination of local campaigns targeting IGSA contracts, state-level

---

22 Carlos Ballesteros, "As Illinois Bans Immigration Detention, One Indiana County Looks to Cash In," *Injustice Watch*, October 12, 2021, injusticewatch.org.

legislation banning detention, and national coordination, the immigration detention system has shrunk for the first time in forty years. Biden reduced the capacity to 25,000 beds in his budget request for 2023.[23] Sustained efforts that required nimbleness among local organizers and advocates have complicated ICE's strategy of having at least one large-capacity, immigrant-only detention center in every region in the US.

In the Midwest, for example, ICE has been trying to build a large jail dedicated to immigrants for over a decade. A coalition of local organizations across the region have played a successful game of whack-a-mole, where anytime a new site is proposed, organizers and advocates work with the local community to make the case against a new detention center. This strategy has worked to stop expansion in at least seven locations near Chicago. In 2012, when ICE first proposed expansion in Crete, a suburb of Chicago, the Illinois Coalition for Immigrant and Refugee Rights (ICIRR) worked with local residents to block the proposal. They used a range of strategies including phone banking, yard signs, rallies, vigils, petitions, and regular engagement with local officials. Research and public-records requests were also an important part of the strategy. With more knowledge about the contract negotiations, activists were better equipped to understand the decision-makers and points of intervention. Once Crete rejected the proposal, ICE went to more towns in Illinois and northern Indiana. Additional groups joined the efforts to stop detention expansion, including Chicago-based organizations, the National Immigrant Justice Center, and Organized Communities Against Deportations.

In 2019, ICE tried to secure a new private detention center in Dwight, a small town an hour south of Chicago. Despite considerable opposition, the city approved the IGSA contract, which would provide it a dollar a day per bed occupied at the proposed 1,200-bed private detention center. However, ICIRR

---

23 Eileen Sullivan, "Biden to Ask Congress for 9,000 Fewer Immigration Detention Beds," *New York Times*, March 25, 2022, nytimes.com.

and others had also been working to get a private detention ban passed through the state legislature; they succeeded, and the ban went into effect shortly after Dwight agreed to the new detention center, blocking the expansion.[24] Even with this victory, Illinois still had IGSAs to detain immigrants at three county jails: Kankakee, McHenry, and Pulaski Counties. Through the Illinois Way Forward Act, passed in 2021, IGSA contracts were also eliminated. Kankakee County and McHenry County both tried to block the legislation through litigation citing the loss of revenue. McHenry County was particularly invested in keeping its contract with ICE, since it had expanded the jail with funds from the federal government, approved in 2004, specifically earmarked to detain immigrants and others for ICE and USMS. However, the case was dismissed, and after over a decade of strategic campaigns involving statewide and local organizing, Illinois no longer detains immigrants for ICE.[25] Five additional states have passed anti-detention laws resulting in terminations of IGSAs.

Many immigration lawyers and advocates are concerned that eliminating IGSAs in some locations will simply drive detention to more conservative states where ending detention is less politically viable. In 2018, attorneys with the New York Immigrant Family Unity Project (NYIFUP), a legal service provider for detained New Yorkers, released a statement against ending the ICE contract at the Hudson County Jail in New Jersey, where New Yorkers were often detained. The group argued that detention near cities was ultimately better and therefore keeping the contract was the more humane option, stating: "we strongly support the movement to abolish ICE ...

24 Illinois Coalition for Immigrant and Refugee Rights, "General Assembly Approves Ban on Private Detention Facilities in Illinois," May 16, 2019, icirr.org.

25 Robert McCoppin, "Lawsuit That Sought to Keep McHenry, Kankakee County Jails for Immigration Detainees Dismissed," *Chicago Tribune*, December 7, 2021, chicagotribune.com.

That said, ending contracts for ICE detention in jails near large immigrant communities where attorneys are provided for free … will do far more harm than good and we question whether directly impacted people were engaged in this decision."[26] Many immigrant rights advocates in the city, even those in favor of abolition, hesitated to support ending the contract because of the concerns raised by the lawyers' statement, and Hudson County reversed its decision to end the contract. After considerable organizing by the growing coalition, Abolish ICE NY-NJ, and staff of NYIFUP-affiliated organizations, many advocates reversed their position. Eventually Hudson relented and ended ICE detention at the county jail.

While the potential for detention expansion elsewhere is always a possibility, the groundswell of grassroots organizing and local campaigns against detention has successfully shifted the national discourse on the issue and led to federal intervention in places like Etowah County, Alabama, and other conservative localities that were less likely to end contracts on their own.[27] The strategy to end IGSAs has proven to be effective at limiting detention and deportation in places with large immigrant populations like California and New Jersey. In fact, and in part because of successful local campaigns to end ICE collaboration with local police and county jails, interior enforcement has subsided considerably since the Obama and Trump administrations.[28] However, the Biden administration has recently started ramping up interior enforcement actions,

---

26 New York Immigrant Family Unity Project, "NYC Public Defenders Implore Hudson County Executive to Postpone Vote on Phase-Out of Hudson County Jail Contract with ICE," September 11, 2018, bronx defenders.org.

27 Maria Sachetti and Nick Miroff, "ICE to Withdraw Immigrant Detainees from Jails in Two States," *Washington Post*, March 25, 2022, washingtonpost.com.

28 Nick Miroff and Maria Sachetti, "ICE Report Shows Sharp Drop in Deportations, Immigration Arrests under Biden," *Washington Post*, March 11, 2022, washingtonpost.com.

making it clear that defending these wins will be critical as immigrant communities continue to be scapegoated and criminalized by both Republicans and Democrats.

Tactical Limitations and Looking Ahead

The strategy of focusing on IGSAs has resulted in major breakthroughs for the movement to end immigration detention. These have been productive campaigns that have shifted the national landscape and reduced the capacity for immigration detention. But if the goal is to dismantle jails and prisons in the US, our work to end detention will require broader shifts to bridge with organizations working to end pretrial detention. The current strategy doesn't consider the necessary shifts needed to combat criminalization and the dependence many counties now have on a carceral economy.

In the most direct limitation, ICE can just circumvent the IGSA strategy, especially in the case of private-prison passthrough contracts like Dilley, where the local government is the intermediary for ICE and private contractors. This happened at the Hutto Detention Center in Taylor, Texas, when, after years of organizing against the jail by women inside and community members, Williamson County commissioners voted to end the IGSA in 2018. ICE signed an emergency one-year contract with CoreCivic, the detention operator, and then secured a 10-year contract despite local opposition.[29] Under Trump, ICE employed this strategy to enter decade-long contracts at detention centers with considerable opposition to ensure that a change in administration would not lead to closures.

While recent wins have ended ICE detention at several county jails, none of these wins have led to facility closure, but have

---

29 Mary Tuma, "ICE Quietly Renews 10-Year Contract with T. Don Hutto Detention Center," *Austin Chronicle*, August 21, 2020, austinchronicle.com.

in fact resulted in new or expanded county jails with increased capacity to lock people up whether for federal agencies, state departments of correction, or nearby counties. The jails remain open, and counties are often strategizing to figure out how to fill empty beds and make up for the lost revenue. Many county jails have underlying USMS contracts, so even though they will no longer detain immigrants for ICE, they will likely still detain immigrants in the custody of USMS who have been prosecuted for immigration violations.

Most critically, anti-detention campaigns, following the dominant script of the immigrant rights movement, have often reinforced criminalizing frames, emphasizing "innocent" immigrants who are not deserving of incarceration in order to argue against ICE detention. This framework not only fails to make the connections between the immigration enforcement and criminal punishment systems, it maintains that county jails are necessary, hurting our ability to make the case against all pretrial detention. Fighting county jail contracts is a critical tool for disrupting the deportation machine. It can and should also be seen as a bridge between migrant justice and carceral abolition movements. Only then will we be on the path toward reversing the jail boom and freeing people from cages.

4

Decarcerating Sacramento: Confronting Jail Expansion in California's Capital

Liz Blum

It all started at a queer bar. Our county was planning a major jail expansion project and we were outraged. A few days later, as the sun set on a warm Friday evening in June 2019, eleven people gathered in my living room. With our own scars from the carceral system and a deep love for our community, we formed an infectious, willful defiance.[1] We knew what was necessary and possible, and we began organizing against Sacramento County's jail expansion.

California's Public Safety Realignment, beginning in 2011, presented new consequences and opportunities for grassroots abolitionist organizers. This shift in sentencing for certain convictions from state prisons to county jails changed the carceral geography of California. It opened new fronts to the struggle for abolition, presenting local communities with new responsibilities to confront jail expansion on the local level. Organizers in Sacramento County were uniquely positioned to do this, and our story provides a specific, and replicable,

---

[1] Shange describes willful defiance as an abolitionist ethos that privileges the necessary over the possible, challenging the legitimacy of the state and its effects. See Savannah Shange, *Progressive Dystopia: Abolition, Antiblackness, and Schooling in San Francisco* (Durham, NC: Duke University Press, 2019).

example of abolitionist organizing in a post-Realignment era, where local municipalities have become new sites of unchecked, carceral growth.

The crisis of what Sacramento County's own consultants name as "over-incarceration"[2] is connected to broader histories of California's prison-building boom and national incarceration trends. California built twenty-three new prisons from 1982 to 2002, setting the world record for prison-building.[3] This state-level prison-building spree occurred alongside significant divestment from social services, which opened pathways for surplus capital to invest in municipal bonds for prison construction.[4] But as capital investment in building state prisons slowed, local cities and counties emerged as a new geography ripe for carceral expansion.

This new landscape has been fueled by jail conditions, litigation, economic incentives, and narratives of carceral humanism. These constitute three central tools—law, capital, and ideology —that were used to justify the growth of jail space in Sacramento County. By addressing these unique drivers of carceral expansion, members of Decarcerate Sacramento—a multiracial coalition of community members, students, lawyers, doctors, parents, data scientists, writers, poets, artists, and friends— fought to accomplish what many said was impossible.

Our first campaign against jail expansion in Sacramento County began with the Rio Cosumnes Correctional Center (RCCC). Sparked by a funding opportunity from the state and further justified by county leadership's use of carceral humanism

---

2 In 2017, Sacramento County's incarceration rate was 47 percent higher than other California counties of similar populations. See Mark Carey and Susan Burke, *Sacramento County Consultant Report on Jail Alternatives* (Carey Group, May 2020), 4, dhs.saccounty.net.

3 Ruth Wilson Gilmore, *Golden Gulag: Prisons, Surplus, Crisis, and Opposition in Globalizing California* (Berkeley: University of California Press, 2007).

4 Ibid.

rhetoric, this project had been in motion for more than five years. We stopped the RCCC expansion project in November 2019, months before the county settled the *Lorenzo Mays, et al. v. County of Sacramento* class-action lawsuit against the Sacramento County Main Jail. Local officials leveraged this lawsuit to push for jail expansion. In response, Decarcerate Sacramento built a campaign against the proposed Main Jail "Annex"—the county's solution to the deadly conditions exposed by the Mays lawsuit. By challenging the county's attempt to instrumentalize the lawsuit toward expansion and centering impacted voices, we successfully pressured the board to vote against the second jail expansion project in March 2021. But our fight to prevent jail expansion in Sacramento County continues.

Budgetary Violence: Realignment & SB1022

The air force base surrounded by farmland in Elk Grove, California, was gifted to Sacramento County in 1960, and became the Rio Cosumnes Correctional Center (RCCC)—the county's second jail. The RCCC jail expansion project began in 2014, when the county applied for bond funding from California Senate Bill 1022, one of many post-Realignment bills allocating funding for jail expansion. Realignment shifted where one would serve their sentence for "non-violent, non-serious, non-sexual" convictions, from state prisons to county jails. This "realignment" solidified the expanding role of the county jail in the carceral state,[5] allocating hundreds of millions in funding to expand local carceral systems.[6]

---

5 Judah Schept, *Progressive Punishment: Job Loss, Jail Growth, and the Neoliberal Logic of Carceral Expansion* (New York: New York University Press, 2015).

6 Pew Charitable Trusts, "Local Spending on Jails Tops $25 Billion in Latest Nationwide Data: Costs Increased Despite Falling Crime and Fewer People Being Admitted to Jail," issue brief, January 29, 2021, pewtrusts.org.

The US Supreme Court lawsuit *Brown v. Plata* ordered that the State of California could no longer build its way out of its prison problems—it had to do something else. That something else was Public Safety Realignment, which passed in 2011 and laid the groundwork for jail expansion projects across the state. More than 175,000 people were sentenced to county jails instead of state prisons in the eight years following the bill.[7] As court processes have slowed over the past decade, it has become normalized for unconvicted individuals to wait years for their cases to be resolved. In Sacramento County, the sentenced population remains insignificant relative to the 83 percent of the 2022 jail population incarcerated with no conviction.

In a post-Realignment era, local governments have been given access to seemingly endless streams of finance capital for carceral expansion, and the agency to decide whether to sell these bonds. In order to prevent the threat of deepening budget austerity, or as Decarcerate Sacramento often called it, budgetary violence, communities within California's fifty-eight counties required their own local, organized opposition to jail expansion.

The bills following Realignment not only drastically increased the availability of capital for carceral expansion at the county level, but specifically offered lease revenue bonds (LRBs), which opened more pathways for the financial sector to capitalize public debt. Lease revenue bonds allow governments to expedite major construction projects by removing the requirement of voter approval and are one of the most expensive loans a county can receive. As high-risk financial instruments, LRBs cost about twice the face value of the original bond, ultimately costing much more than traditional general obligation bonds.[8] Unlike

---

7 Abbie Vansickle and Manuel Villa, "Who Begs to Go to Prison? California Jail Inmates," *Marshall Project*, April 23, 2019, themarshall project.org.

8 "AB900 Borrows $7.5 Billion to Build New Prisons: Fact Sheet on the Use of Lease Revenue Bonds to Build Prisons," Californians United for a Responsible Budget, May 2008, curbprisonspending.org.

projects like bridges where the lessee can generate revenues post-completion to finance the debt, the RCCC jail expansion would have incentivized Sacramento County to allocate more funding to the sheriff for more staffing and ongoing operating costs created by new building construction.

This restructuring of local government finance toward a reliance on public debt shifts the political accountability to creditors and away from local residents.[9] The financing of carceral construction projects through LRBs functions as a way for the ruling class to exploit local austerity policies as a means to transfer public money into the private sector.[10] By calling the SB1022 lease revenue bond a grant, Sacramento County executive staff attempted to conceal the reality of LRBs, which have historically been used as a political tactic created to build state prisons without voter approval.[11]

Decarcerate Sacramento challenged county staff's renaming of the LRB as a "grant from the state" and exposed that the bond would lock the county into the ongoing fiscal cost of operating the jail. In a local context of increasing austerity, where carceral spending has been prioritized over public health for decades,[12] organizers stressed that accepting the bond would eliminate any incentive to decrease the number of people in the county's overcrowded jails. The financial commitment to the SB1022 LRB would have required the county to operate the jail for at least thirty years, further entrenching the policing

9 Wang explains that this model of public finance, which increasingly relies on borrowing rather than taxation, "creates a situation where creditors, rather than the public, become the privileged constituency of governments." See Jackie Wang, *Carceral Capitalism* (South Pasadena, CA: Semiotext(e), 2018), 71.

10 Gilmore, *Golden Gulag.*

11 Ibid.

12 See Jason Pohl and Alexandra Yoon-Hendricks, "Sacramento County Public Health Lab Faced Years of Budget Cuts. Then Came the COVID-19 Pandemic," *Sacramento Bee,* April 27, 2020, sacbee.com.

and incarcerating of primarily Black and Brown Sacramento County residents.[13]

Through public comments at Sacramento County Board of Supervisors' meetings, community members provided impactful analysis and personal experiences that exposed budgetary violence. Kirin Rajagopalan, a graduate student and organizer with Critical Resistance, stated that "this $500M jail expansion project, regardless of its re-bid, is a simplistic, violent and counterproductive way of addressing complex issues of houselessness, mental health, and poverty which will further exacerbate the stark material, racial, and economic disparities in this county for decades to come." Khalil Ferguson, CEO at United CORE Alliance, said in response to the county's attempts to argue that this project would help meet the *Mays* consent decree, "The argument that the county will avoid incurring costs from the lawsuit is negated by the fact that the county will not avoid incurring costs from SB1022," adding that "the motive for this jail expansion is not to deal with individuals within a carceral system but more the colonial state using its incentive to generate profit for private corporations." Community members like Ferguson further exposed the realities of lease revenue bonds and called for the rejection of the fiscally violent proposal rooted in racial capitalism.

The economic impacts of this proposal could not be separated from the budget cuts that communities across the county were facing. Jay Franco, an organizer with Sac Kids First, noted that "tonight there are schools proposed to be closed, and jails proposed to be expanded." He asked, "What type of world do we bring youth in where the jail system is the largest public housing facility in the county?" Dozens of public commenters stressed the need to invest in community services instead of investing in jails.

---

13 The Sacramento County jail population is consistently 37 percent Black, while the population of Black people in Sacramento County is just under 11 percent.

In the months following the successful cancellation of the RCCC project on November 5, 2019, Sacramento County CEO Nav Gill and his staff, with support from Scott Jones, then the Sacramento County sheriff, tried to pressure the Board to reverse its decision. The Board of Supervisors was presented with a Grand Jury report in September 2020, less than a year after organizers stopped the RCCC expansion project.[14] The report recommended that the County "reconsider" its decision to reject the SB1022 "grant," with a letter of support from Sheriff Scott Jones stating "without new capital improvement to RCCC, the County of Sacramento will be unable to meet the expectations set forth in the *Mays* Consent Decree."[15] The sheriff's claim to be unable to improve jail conditions without the jail expansion weaponized his independent elected power, and threatened to impede the county's ability to meet legal standards of care for people incarcerated in its jails.

Attempting to rewrite history and erase the impacts of local abolitionist organizing, the sheriff explained that "the report included findings and recommendations based on the Grand Jury's investigation into the County of Sacramento's *reluctance* to accept the $80 million in related funding from SB1022."[16] The County CEO's response to the grand jury report, "California Senate Bill 1022: A Gift Too Good to Ignore," urged the Board of Supervisors to reconsider its decision to reject the SB1022 lease revenue bond before an upcoming state deadline to accept the funds.[17] But the board turned him down.

Decarcerate Sacramento's community organizing exposed the relationship between the proposed bond acceptance and

14 Sacramento County Grand Jury, "California Senate Bill 1022: A Gift Too Good to Ignore," Sacramento Superior Court, 2020, saccourt.ca.gov.

15 Scott R. Jones, "Response from Sacramento County Sheriff's Office," letter to Judge Russell Hom, July 27, 2020, sacgrandjury.org.

16 Ibid.

17 Sacramento County Grand Jury, "California Senate Bill 1022."

ongoing operational cost of the project with the threat of increased social divestment that would deepen racial disparities in the county. Sacramento County is one of only four counties in California to abandon plans for new jails.[18] Unfortunately, the rejection of LRB funding in this county allowed these unspent funds to be used for other jail expansion projects in other counties throughout California. Organizers at the state level have advocated for this jail funding to be made available for non-carceral projects but have so far been unsuccessful.

While state laws created the economic incentives that prompted the RCCC expansion project, the absence of a specific legal mandate incentivized the county's decision to build or not to build. The following proposal to expand the downtown jail, however, presented more complex challenges. Organizers could no longer rely solely on the budgetary violence of jail expansion; we had to reckon with the complex legal requirements for the physical space inside the county's jails.

Jail Conditions Litigation:
The *Mays v. Sacramento* Lawsuit

The *Lorenzo Mays, et al. v. County of Sacramento* class-action lawsuit was finalized in January 2020, requiring the county to meet legal standards for medical and mental health care, suicide prevention, use of solitary confinement, disability rights (ADA), and medical privacy (HIPAA). This lawsuit was the central catalyst and ultimately the core justification for the proposed new "annex" of the Sacramento County Main Jail.[19]

---

18 Jacob Kang-Brown et al., "Stop Fueling Jail Construction in California and Invest in Community-Based Services," fact sheet, Vera Institute of Justice, February 2021, https://vera-advocacy-and-partnerships.s3.amazonaws.com/ca/California-Jail-Construction-2021.pdf.

19 Tifanei Ressl-Moyer, Pilar Gonzalez Morales, and Jaqueline Aranda Osorno, "Movement Lawyering During a Crisis: How the Legal

When confronted with conditions litigation, government officials have overwhelmingly chosen to increase spending on incarceration even when other more humane and cost-effective solutions exist.[20] Prison and jail conditions lawsuits continue to provide a perfect bureaucratic pretext for government officials to justify expanding the physical space of their cages. But as the *Mays* consent decree makes clear, the policies and behavior of jail staff are the true causes of the unlivable conditions inside Sacramento County jails.

The campaign to stop the expansion of the Main Jail was built upon the organizing that successfully canceled the RCCC jail expansion in 2019. We knew that the lawsuit did not require a new building, but that the plan to build a "Correctional Health and Mental Health Facility" was borne directly from conversations with attorneys on both sides of the class-action lawsuit, and county officials who convinced themselves that the only way to meet the *Mays* consent decree was to expand.[21]

System Exploits the Labor of Activists and Undermines Movements," *City University of New York Law Review* 24, no. 1 (2021): 91.

20 William D. Duncombe and Jeffrey D. Straussman. "The Impact of Courts on the Decision to Expand Jail Capacity," *Administration and Society* 25, no. 3 (1993): 267–92; Joshua Guetzkow and Eric Schoon, "If You Build It, They Will Fill It: The Consequences of Prison Overcrowding Litigation," *Law and Society Review* 49, no. 2 (2015): 401–32; Heather Schoenfeld, "Mass Incarceration and the Paradox of Prison Conditions Litigation," *Law and Society Review* 44, no. 3–4 (2010): 731–68. See also Ressl-Moyer et al., "Movement Lawyering During a Crisis."

21 "The Prison Law Office said the consent decree does not necessarily require Sacramento County to build or expand its jail facilities to address its lack of mental health services. Though creating a new facility is one option, 'on the other hand they could reduce the jail population significantly to allow for staff to provide care to existing facilities'" (Alexandra Yoon-Hendricks, "Sacramento County CA Jail Expansion Stopped after Protests," *Sacramento Bee*, November 7, 2019, sacbee. com). While this sentiment was reiterated in private meetings throughout the jail fights, the litigants chose never to speak publicly in county hearings on their positions, despite requests by organizers.

Court-appointed investigators exposed how jail staff continued to make insignificant progress on consent decree requirements, which in turn continued to cause preventable suffering and deaths.[22] All eleven monitoring reports published as of 2022 provide scathing evidence of jail management's "deeply concerning" failure to ensure that jail staff are following their own protocols.[23] They explained that staffing shortages are "endemic" to the jails, which further supported our calls to reduce the jail population in order to lower patient-staffing ratios.[24]

Decarcerate Sacramento stressed that conditions needed to improve urgently, and that jail population reduction was the only possible solution. We explained to the county and the public that the expansion plan offered a false promise—it would not address policies, procedures, training, and staff compliance with policies inside. A building is just a building. One report recognized that "the future MJ Annex building seems to be the answer everyone is counting on," while the vast majority of changes required by the *Mays* consent decree are unrelated to building structure. The proposed building would also take at least five years to complete—well outside the legal deadlines of the consent decree, but silently deemed acceptable under the violent bureaucratic process of meeting the lowest minimum standards of civil rights law.

---

22 More than a year after approval of the consent decree, the county had achieved substantial compliance on only 5 percent of medical provisions, none of the mental health provisions, and none of the suicide prevention provisions of the remedial plan.

23 Mary Perrien, "First Report of Compliance in Mental Health Services Based on Consent Decree," *Mays et al v Sacramento County* Case No. 2:18-cv-02081-TLN-KJN, January 20, 2021, PDF available at disabilityrightsca.org.

24 "Second Monitoring Report on Restrictive Housing, Discipline, and Classification Practices in the Sacramento County Jails," *Mays v. County of Sacramento* Case No. 18-02081, July 2022, 31, PDF available at disabilityrightsca.org.

In April 2020, the Board of Supervisors made their first significant public decision on the Main Jail expansion plan, awarding a $7 million architectural contract to start designing the annex. At the hearing, Supervisor Patrick Kennedy (a "progressive" Democrat) asked county executive staff rhetorically if "the plaintiffs on the case would see, if we didn't move forward on this, a lack of commitment to the case and meeting its obligations?" Supervisor Susan Peters (a conservative Republican) further justified approval by stating that "this is an important moment to demonstrate our commitment to upholding the legal settlement that we entered into." With no opportunity for public comment during the meeting, the motion passed unanimously, entering the county into a contract with the architecture firm Nacht & Lewis to begin designing the project. This architectural contract would later become a primary tool used by county staff to justify the project even after the board voted against it.

The *Mays* lawsuit requires compliance with the Americans with Disabilities Act (ADA) and the Health Insurance Portability and Accountability Act (HIPAA), especially in the jail's intake and booking area. These two laws emerged as the most significant in our fight to prove that the consent decree did not require a new building. Reducing the jail population, also required by the consent decree, would make more space available to meet HIPAA and ADA requirements, but the county refused to seriously consider that possibility. Nacht & Lewis reported that there was no way to widen doorways or cells in the current jail to meet the ADA. With no peer review from any impartial architecture firm, it's difficult to know if this is true, but the county's second jail facility (RCCC) already met most ADA requirements. Sacramento County leadership could choose to use the rural RCCC jail to meet the *Mays* consent decree, but they were unwilling to entertain an option that would inconvenience law enforcement.

The court-appointed monitors outlined how jail staff should use the existing spaces in the Main Jail for HIPAA compliance.

For example, medical and mental health staff can utilize sound-proof interview booths or classroom space for confidential patient conversations. But investigations found that jail staff were not using these existing options, and even when they did, custody staff would not close the door. Organizers stressed that a new building will never guarantee that jail staff will make use of space in a way that protects the privacy or disability rights of those incarcerated.

Decarcerate Sacramento spent the following months organizing: educating the community through public forums and social media and meeting with county supervisors, county staff, allied architects, and *Mays* plaintiff's counsel. We gathered information through careful research of all publicly available *Mays* legal documents and strategic relationship building that informed our campaign strategy toward the ultimate goal of convincing the county to meet the consent decree without a new building.

Meeting the *Mays* consent decree became the center of nearly every conversation about the Main Jail expansion. The *Mays* plaintiff's counsel, made up of three law firms who represent everyone incarcerated in Sacramento County jails, were a critical piece of swaying the board's decision. Plaintiff's counsel was weaponized by the county's legal team, and their opinions were falsely represented. In a final effort to convince the board to move forward with the project at the March 2021 hearing, County Counsel Lisa Travis said that plaintiff's attorneys "did not call in," and "they didn't oppose this project ... They believe this is a project that will help us get to the consent decree." Travis stated as if it were fact that "there is certainly risk of upsetting plaintiff's counsel and upsetting the consent decree by not taking this action." This heavy-handed advocacy by county counsel foreshadows the efforts of county staff to continue the project even after the board's decision.

Decarcerate Sacramento's public education work made clear that in order to meet the consent decree the county would have to address structural and systemic process issues by changing policies, organizational leadership, and accountability structures. On March 10, 2021, after many hours of powerful testimony against jail expansion, community members successfully pressured the board to cancel the project and focus on reducing the jail population to comply with the consent decree.

Carceral Humanism: Centering Impacted Voices

By deploying dangerous narratives of incarceration as a place for "rehabilitation" and "treatment," supporters of expansion are trying to repackage jails and prisons as capable of being more than spaces of punishment and control.[25] This concept has been termed carceral humanism, which emerged as a central focus of our narrative-shifting strategy in the fight against jail expansion.[26]

Rallying cries of "Can't Get Well in a Cell" and "Care, Not Cages" echoed throughout the campaigns to stop both jail expansions. Carceral humanism was central to the county's justification for both jail expansion projects, but especially in their proposed expansion of the Sacramento County Main Jail.[27] Emphasizing its moral and legal commitment to better medical and mental health care in the jail, the county planned to build what it called a "Correctional Health and Mental Health Services Facility," or what was more aptly named by organizers as a "Mental Health Jail." But even the *Mays* lawsuit investigators urged the county to invest in community-based mental health treatment to stop the cycle of incarceration. In

---

25 Mariame Kaba, *We Do This 'Til We Free Us: Abolitionist Organizing and Transforming Justice* (Chicago: Haymarket Books, 2021); Maya Schenwar and Vikki Law, *Prison by Any Other Name: The Harmful Consequences of Popular Reforms* (New York: New Press, 2020); Gilmore, *Golden Gulag*; Schept, *Progressive Punishment.*

26 James Kilgore, "Repackaging Mass Incarceration," *CounterPunch*, June 6, 2014, counterpunch.org.

27 Ibid.

Sacramento County, 57 percent of those arrested are released within three days, and the vast majority of people arrested have been diagnosed with a mental illness.[28]

As Niki Jones, who had been incarcerated during mental health crises, said in a Decarcerate Sacramento press release ahead of the vote on the Main Jail expansion, "It was not the building that made it harder for me; it was the sheriffs." Pamela Emanual, who was incarcerated in the Main Jail for nearly three years said: "It was the cruel way they treated you—in constant isolation, locking you down like an animal. Even with the consent decree in place they continued to do that. They never stopped." Emanual emphasized that "the space is not the problem; it's the management." Centering the expertise of people who have been incarcerated in Sacramento County jails further refuted narratives of carceral humanism.

In addition to the experiences of those who had been incarcerated in the jails and their loved ones, health professionals who had worked inside the county jails also played a key role in refuting narratives of carceral humanism. MK Orsulak, a primary care physician, stressed: "This jail expansion will … in no way lead to ethical medicine. There is no way ethical medicine can be practiced in what is being proposed right now." Asantewaa Boykin, co-founder of the Anti-Police-Terror Project and a registered nurse, told the board: "Handcuffs are not therapeutic. Forced compliance does not equal wellness." She added that as an RN she has "seen compassion and resources be more effective than some medications." Dr. Christina Bourne, a psychiatry and family medicine resident who had worked inside the Main Jail, said that a more "therapeutic" architectural design "is not going to solve the root causes of the consent decree and of suffering inside. An 'improved facility' will not solve the systemic and cultural issues of sheriff deputy behavior and abuse." Public testimony from doctors and nurses who had

---

28 Perrien, "First Report of Compliance in Mental Health Services."

worked with incarcerated populations provided direct contradiction to county staff's claims that the design of the building is causing the dehumanizing jail conditions.

Centering the needs and experiences of people inside the jails also guided the campaign to stop the Main Jail expansion plan. Incarcerated people continued to experience mistreatment caused by the behavior and protocols of jail staff, not by the structure of the buildings. Organizers frequently visited people inside the jail and communicated through phone and writing when the COVID-19 pandemic reached Sacramento County. The abuse shared from inside ranged from the medical abuse of pregnant women, to negligence and torture of people with mental illness, to racist harassment by correctional officers. With consent of individuals and careful consideration of retaliation, organizers shared these experiences with county actors in press releases and in public comments. In centering the voices of those disappeared behind concrete walls that the county claimed to care about, we shifted public discourse.

Organizing with people inside Sacramento County jails became a central tactic. All founding members of Decarcerate Sacramento have experienced incarceration or have had family incarcerated. Our coalition knew that the voices and leadership of people currently locked in Sacramento's cages were, and are, critical to refuting narratives of what would improve conditions inside. In 2019, two Black women inside the Sacramento County Main Jail launched our Inside/Outside organizing work, which has allowed us to build a network of relationships with people inside the jails through writing, visiting, and mutual aid. In July 2022, we launched an official jail hotline. We have humanized issues around jailing through this work, and continue to write op-eds, hold press conferences, and interview with news outlets to present the truth in the public narrative: that incarceration does not make anyone safer.

The campaign to prevent the Main Jail expansion in 2021 revealed that any new building would not change the inherent culture of punishment and abuse that led to the class-action lawsuit. The county's reliance on carceral humanism throughout the campaign shows the county's desire to shift the public's view of the purpose and possibility of jails, beyond punishment and toward humane spaces of care, in an attempt to legitimize the role of jails in communities. Abolitionist organizers must continue to expose that new buildings will not result in better treatment of those locked inside. Only by reducing local jail populations and having local budgets prioritize significant investment in meeting basic human needs will we support people's health and well-being.

Conclusion

This chapter has shown how economic, legal, and ideological conditions created a landscape ripe for carceral expansion in Sacramento County and how local grassroots organizing was required in the face of new threats of capital investment, conditions litigation, and carceral humanism. Despite our success in preventing jail expansion thus far, a constant threat of carceral expansion remains, fueled by the significant growth of fear-based rhetoric and false narratives of safety in local and national news media in recent years. Our work is far from over.

County executives and the sheriff have attempted to revive the canceled jail expansion plans. In 2020, these officials got a grand jury involved to push the board to reverse its cancellation of the RCCC expansion project. After the county Board of Supervisors voted to cancel the Main Jail annex project, county staff changed the scope of work on the architectural firm's contract to complete a "population study" to justify the need for a new building, despite the board's decision to focus on reducing the jail population. Ultimately, unelected county staff have proven unwilling to follow the will of the Board of Supervisors and the community.

Over a year after its historic vote to cancel the Main Jail expansion, the county was just beginning to create its first jail population reduction plan. But before any plans were seriously invested in, the board voted in December 2022 to restart the jail annex project in the name of meeting the *Mays* consent decree. New architectural studies by Nacht & Lewis—funded by their original contract that was never canceled—claimed that even after significant population reduction, building a new jail annex was the only way to meet compliance of ADA and HIPAA laws. The board chose to trust county staff, instead of the community they represent, that all alternative options were fully explored.

The *Mays* lawsuit became the single most catalyzing factor in the county's decision to expand the jail. As abolitionist organizers, we need to confront the harmful and unintended impacts of conditions litigation and work to shift the way the law is used to confront the use of incarceration. Lawyers should also learn from the impacts of the *Mays* lawsuit and wield the law as a tool for strengthening care and social safety nets and permanently shrink carceral systems.

Imagine if consent decrees ordered jail closures and required local governments to build preventative and alternative non-carceral infrastructure in communities. This future is possible, and it starts with telling our stories.

5

"Not One More Dollar Goes into This Jail": Becoming Abolitionists in Upstate New York

Andrew J. Pragacz and Kevin Revier

Our involvement in the anti-jail expansion movement in Broome County, New York, goes back about a decade. Both of us had recently entered the sociology graduate program at Binghamton University a year or two removed from finishing undergraduate programs. We were eager to contribute to the program's radical, activist tradition. To name a few actions, in the years prior students had organized the mailing of a magazine written by and for incarcerated people, called *OFF!*; professors had taught volunteer, noncredit classes at New York's infamous Elmira maximum security prison after the state terminated all higher education prison-based programs in 1995; students and faculty for ten years went with the university's Black Student Union on visits to an upstate youth prison; another professor worked with an NAACP-led effort to document medical abuses in the jail and to jumpstart a reentry program;[1] a group of university professors and students met for several years with other community members under the banner of the Binghamton Justice Projects to discuss issues within the criminal legal system; and several other graduate

---

1 Joshua M. Price, *Prison and Social Death* (New Brunswick, NJ: Rutgers University Press, 2015).

students had been organizing against policing and criminalization in Binghamton.[2]

In 2014 we jumped into the fight by helping to kickstart a belated effort to prevent a $6.8 million expansion of the Broome County jail. A year later, in the 2015 Black Lives Matter summer, we helped found a community organization to continue this work, called Justice and Unity in the Southern Tier (JUST). JUST is dedicated to dismantling mass incarceration and mass policing in the Binghamton area, and advocating for and with incarcerated people, their families, and their loved ones. Under the JUST banner we have held dozens of protests, started a jail visiting program, conducted and published research, held community forums, met with county, state, and local officials and office seekers, testified to county and state legislatures, and worked with other community organizations advocating for those with disabilities, mental health, and substance use issues. From these experiences we arrived at the conclusion that no money should ever, for any reason, be allocated to the jail or police.

The particulars of incarceration in Broome County are unique, but the pattern of economic decline and incarceration is hardly novel to mid-size and small urban areas in the rust belt. In the early 20th century, the county's economy was anchored by industrial manufacturing and the white-collar workers who managed those enterprises. Welfare capitalist (and virulently anti-union) firms like the Endicott-Johnson Shoe Company and IBM dominated local employment. Although deindustrialization started in the 1960s, the defense industry kept Broome County humming through the 1980s. The end of the Cold War and the implementation of the North American Free Trade Agreement (NAFTA) swept away the remaining industrial base. As jobs and factories left, so did the population. From 1970 to the late 2010s, Broome County lost approximately

2 Brendan McQuade was working on a dissertation at Binghamton during this time which would culminate in Brendan McQuade, *Pacifying the Homeland* (Oakland: University of California Press, 2019).

30,000 people, over 10 percent of the 1970 population. In an era of wage stagnation, wage growth has been even slower in Binghamton. Today the county's poverty is 50 percent above the national average and is behind only the Bronx in New York State.[3] It is double for Black and Latinx people in the county, who make up 7 percent and 5 percent of the population respectively. Homelessness doubled between 2010 and 2020.

Like many other deindustrialized areas in the US, the county has relied on expanding government- and state-funded initiatives, big-box retailers, and health care to maintain some semblance of its old tax base. Approximately 20 percent of all jobs are government employment, and jobs in the criminal legal system—for example, police and correctional officers—are seen by many working-class people as desirable and decent-paying with good health-care benefits and the promise of a pension.[4] County jobs that pay in six figures are overwhelmingly correctional officer positions. By 2016, Broome County had the highest jail incarceration rate of any county in the state; the jail held, on average, 39 of every 100,000 people in the county, over twice the rate of New York City.[5] Meanwhile, county legislators closed the regional mental health center and have continuously cut funding for health care. Police ferry people to an emergency-room mental health crisis unit while courts provide access to substance use treatment services through surveillance-based programing, with jail time for inevitable stumbles. Structurally, the jail papers over the ever-growing "service gaps" through its warehousing function.

---

3 Office of the New York State Comptroller, "New Yorkers in Need: A Look at Poverty Trends in New York State for the Last Decade" (2022).

4 Bureau of Labor Statistics, "Economy at a Glance: Binghamton, NY," 2023, bls.gov.

5 Jack Norton, "'We Are Not Going to Rest': Organizing Against Incarceration in Upstate New York," *In Our Backyards Stories*, September 3, 2019, vera.org.

Our first efforts to prevent a jail expansion were a failure. The jail expansion went forward with only minor dissent in the county legislature, prompted by a poorly organized protest action. The defeat left us angry and confused, but motivated and curious: why was our local jail expanding when imprisonment was falling in New York State? Why were legislators willing to continue dumping money in the jail when more than 70 percent of the people incarcerated were being held pretrial? We spent two years looking at these questions from an academic perspective, ultimately culminating in a book, *After Prisons? Freedom, Decarceration, and Justice Disinvestment* (2016). At the same time we began meeting with other community members and became increasingly concerned about medical abuses at the Broome County Jail, the staggering number of jail deaths (twelve have died since 2011), the high number of detained and incarcerated people, and the racialized nature of this incarceration (while Black people account for 7 percent of the county population, they make up over 30 percent of the people in jail).

The first big advocacy push organized by JUST revealed the political contradictions of those years as we built an organization capable of amassing support from the public, nonprofits, and elected officials. We wanted reductions in the number of people subject to punitive state interventions *and* we wanted those who did experience jailing to be treated better, which in turn meant increasing health services in the jail. In early 2017, JUST produced an action plan, titled "Less Death and More Health: An Action Plan for Broome County." We demanded a 50 percent reduction in the number of persons incarcerated in the jail, especially for people with mental illness and substance use issues, as well as greater use of Release on Recognizance (ROR) and reductions in the use of solitary confinement. Yet, we also made medical demands that could too easily be co-opted for expanded carceral power and jail funding. Although we were consistent in arguing for reductions in jail budgets and staffing, we also supported *improved* mental health resources with "proper funding;" and we advocated for medication-assisted treatment (MAT) like methadone and Suboxone, which was opposed by both the jail's medical provider and the sheriff. We also demanded better mental and physical health evaluations. At rallies, we offered uncritical endorsements of replacing cops with social workers and mental health professionals alongside calls for "alternatives to incarceration." In our initial documents we professed an "all-of-the-above" anti–mass incarceration strategy, uncomfortably appropriating the Obama administration's domestic energy production policy just as the victorious (for now) anti-fracking movement was winding down in New York State. In retrospect, these demands look naïve and were even at odds with our stated goal to shrink the size and power of the jail.

We should have known better: the rhetoric of improved healthcare had already been used to justify the 2014 expansion, which included a "state of the art" sixteen-bed medical unit. The sheriff, David Harder, who at the time insisted the state forced him to do this, began to proclaim that the additional space would accommodate those incarcerated with "heroin problems" and "hard mental problems."[6] When the State Senate's Heroin Task Force approved $4 million for addiction services in the state's jails, with $400,000 going to Broome County, the area's state senator at the time, Republican Fred Akshar, offered a sympathetic view of those incarcerated. "It's incumbent upon us," he said, "to provide the most basic of human services to people."[7] This rhetoric was—and still is—hard to challenge. (Akshar became the Broome County sheriff in 2023.)

The abuses continued. While detoxing from heroin in isolation, Lisa, a woman we interviewed, was harassed by a guard

6 John R. Roby, "Broome Plans 13 Deputies for Jail," Press Connects, September 27, 2015, pressconnects.com.

7 "State Senate Approves Plan to Add Addiction Services to Jail," Spectrum News, June 21, 2018, spectrumlocalnews.com.

who asked her: "How are those fuckin' drugs treating you now?" And as those who have written to us professed, guards and medical providers routinely withheld prescriptions, including for insulin, inhalers, and blood-pressure medication. Taej'on Vega was denied prescribed Adderall, Geodon, Lexapro, and Risperdal. In his legal complaint, Mr. Vega offers a traumatizing "shakedown," where he was beaten, strip-searched, harassed, and abused with racial slurs.[8] Rob Card, who was jailed for a drug court violation, was denied medical care despite having a brain tumor. Unable to walk, he fell numerous times and had ongoing seizures. The jail released him, removing him from custody and off the county's tab. He was pronounced dead in the hospital following a grand mal seizure he had in custody.[9] No state investigation was conducted. Placing a container of Rob's ashes on the table during one of our meetings, his sister, determined to fight back, proclaimed, "We have to do something."[10] Thomas Husar, a man with systemic mastocytosis, died while jailed for a probation violation. In the twelve hours before his death, according to a lawsuit filed by his family, he repeatedly pleaded for assistance to indifferent guards. His family had contacted the jail when he was first incarcerated and was assured by jail administrators he'd be looked out for.

In touring the facility, advocates Judy Arnold and Alexis Pleus described another area of abuse—sexual voyeurism and violence in the new women's unit, also funded from the 2015 expansion. As they wrote in the local newspaper, "Women sleep in bunks along the walls, eat in the middle of the room at tables just several feet from their beds, shower in stalls with no shower curtain and use open toilets with no walls around them, next

---

8 *"Taej'on Vega v. Broome County, Hrebin, Fowler, Weir,"* Justice and Unity for the Southern Tier, August 26, 2021, justicest.com.

9 Bill Martin, "Rob Card's Death: 'Broome County Is Killing Me,'" *Just Talk* (blog), March 12, 2019, justtalk.blog.

10 Norton, "'We Are Not Going to Rest.'"

to each other and within eyeshot of where people sit to eat."[11] Incarcerated women have reported miscarriages and a lack of access to pads, tampons, and bras at the jail. We interviewed a woman, pregnant when incarcerated, who was told by a corrections officer, "You don't deserve to have a child. I honestly hope that child dies in your stomach because you're gonna have another addict baby who is just like you." Speaking to the NYCLU, Makyla Holland expressed particular abuse being Black and transgender, "I was humiliated by Broome County jail staff because I am a transgender woman. I was harassed, mocked, misgendered, and worse: jail staff strip-searched me, beat me up, placed me in the male section of the jail, and withheld my hormones for a period of time, forcing me to go into agonizing withdrawal."[12]

Despite the rampant abuses and significant media coverage, when we have expressed our concerns to officials, we were ignored. At each step, we were met with condescension, hostility, or vague promises about following up. For years we met with the Democratic county executive to discuss our concerns about the jail and the medical care at the jail. We came to these meetings armed with graphs and studies. Reasoned argument never won the day. Our first meeting was almost canceled because the newly elected county executive did not want to speak with an outspoken advocate for some perceived breach of decorum. The result of all of these meetings was that a new food provider came in—Trinity Services Group—and the mental health piece of the medical care contract was separated out in hopes of encouraging more bids. Trinity was just as bad as the previous vendor, and the medical provider, CMC, got the contract again for both the medical and mental health care.

---

11 Judy Arnold and Alexis Pleus, "Women Have No Privacy in Broome County," Press Connects, March 29, 2018, pressconnects.com.

12 NYCLU, "Transgender Woman Sues Broome County and Broome County Sheriff and Jail Staff for Discrimination, Abuse and Denial of Medical Care," press release, March 29, 2022, nyclu.org.

Since our work began, however, we've seen significant shifts in jail incarceration, thanks in part to the advocacy of organizations like JUST. In 2015, as the jail was being expanded to hold 600 persons, it held 517 a day on average. In January 2023, that number dropped to 296, a 43 percent drop, only 7 percentage points away from the initial target in our first Action Plan.[13] Much of this drop occurred beginning in 2020, but even before the onset of the pandemic and implementation of bail reform in New York State, the jail population had been decreasing. The drop in incarceration rates is promising and our Action Plan and the work that followed were critical interventions exposing the violence of incarceration in Broome County. Besides the falling incarceration rate, the political success of the anti–mass incarceration movement locally has meant that local politicians are forced to take stances on criminal justice issues. Some, like Sheriff Akshar—himself a former sheriff's deputy—seek reformist credentials while others, like his predecessor, double down on tough-on-crime politics.[14]

The impressive reductions in jail incarceration in Broome County and across the state are partial (and potentially fleeting) victories. First, too many people continue to be incarcerated, and over 70 percent of people in the county jail are being held pretrial. Even more significantly, the criminal legal system in Broome County retains the capacity to arrest, prosecute, and incarcerate thousands more people than it currently does. Just because the number of people incarcerated today is lower than in the past does not mean the county can't quickly ramp it back up. Despite the large drop in incarceration, only one pod in the jail has been closed. No money has been clawed back from the criminal legal system and no staffing cuts have been

---

13 New York State Division of Criminal Justice Services, "Monthly Jail Population Trends," criminaljustice.ny.gov.

14 For example, during the 2022 sheriff campaign, Akshar took special care to mention the jail deaths. This exposure was central to JUST's organizing efforts for many years.

made at the jail. While the elimination of cash bail in 2019 made it more difficult to lock up people pretrial, there was no corresponding investment in welfare services or support for impoverished people. And almost as soon as bail reform went into effect, the state *reformed the reform* within a few months, making it easier to incarcerate people thanks to a relentless police-led fear-mongering campaign. And in 2023, New York State rolled back the bail reform even further, giving judges more discretion to lock people up before trial.

Our simple insistence that not a single dollar more should be allocated to the mass incarceration system is critical to the movement moving forward in our region of Upstate New York and nationally. Almost three years after demands to defund the police rang through US cities for a summer of rebellion, the American Rescue Plan Act (ARPA)—passed to assist local governments with COVID-related expenses and to support impacted communities—funneled billions to cops, jails, and courts. Locally, William Martin has found in analyzing ARPA records and county budgets that the Broome County sheriff received an additional $7 million. This after over a decade of continuous growth for the jail budget.[15]

Our region is also seeing a renewed commitment to jailing as a means to provide services. The newly elected sheriff, Akshar, is calling for more funding for expanding jailed-based reentry programming, expanding the office's public relations abilities, filling thirty-eight vacant guard positions, upgrading medical care, and establishing a four-person "Community Response Team [whose] purpose will be to use the integrated community policing model to respond to community conflicts or surges of crime wherever they are presented. Real-time data and input directly from the community will be utilized by this team."[16]

---

15 Bill Martin, "Broome County's ARPA Bonanza: Who Captured the $37 Million?," *Binghamton Bridge*, January 24, 2023, binghamton bridge.org.

16 Ella Michelle Connors, "Sheriff Ashkar Announces New

At the same time, Tompkins County (Ithaca is its county seat), with one of the lowest incarceration rates in New York State, is looking to replace its jail and add a host of services including secure transition housing for those recently released, classroom space, improved medical facilities, and special detox cells. These plans mean more resources, more personnel, and, above all, more money. Both plans will face intense hostility but are likely to manifest in some form. Jail populations have been allowed to fall to increasingly low levels, but state control—through probation, treatment, and the like—has not decreased.

To address the shifting terrain of political struggle compelled by the anti–mass incarceration movement we must now be even clearer that not one more dollar should go to the jail, in any form or fashion. The politics behind our insistence are sometimes messy. While there is an unstable consensus around reducing the number of people incarcerated, stemming the flow of money is a harder political sell. Criminal legal system dollars fund NGOs who provide reentry and treatment services.[17] Not only does it put us out of step with some potential allies, but it is easy to read our position as callous and cruel toward those locked up inside. Even within JUST we've had a long-running debate about giving people commissary. Supporting people inside is an important part of our mission, but a portion of every commissary dollar goes into a sheriff's slush fund.[18] To be sure, we agree that medical prescriptions and services must be available in the jail, but that should not be a reason to criminalize and incarcerate people. Nor is it a reason to keep expanding the jail—which is fundamentally a place of

Community Plan," *Pipe Dream*, February 2, 2023, bupipedream.com.

17 Jarrod Shanahan and Zhandarka Kurti, *States of Incarceration: Rebellion, Reform, and America's Punishment System* (London, Reaktion Books, 2022).

18 Bill Martin, "Broome County Jail's Secret $ Millions: Profiting from COVID and Incarcerated Families," *Just Talk* (blog), June 3, 2022, justtalk.blog.

institutionalized violence and degradation. As fellow activist-scholar Hannah Walter reminds us, jail health care cannot be real health care, as there is no effort to restore physical, mental, or emotional well-being. We maintain that we must tear down carceral structures—by disinvesting from the jail—while building up communities that support the health and well-being for all outside the carceral state. Cut the funding. Raise their costs. Reduce capacity. That is the path to abolition.

6

"You Start with Where You Are and with the People Who Are Around You": Organizing Against Jails Across Tennessee

An Interview with Dawn Harrington and Gicola Lane of Free Hearts

Jack Norton: Can you tell us about Free Hearts and how you came to organizing?

Dawn Harrington: Free Hearts is a statewide organization led by formerly incarcerated women that provides support, education, advocacy, and organizing for families impacted by incarceration. Our ultimate goals are reuniting families and strengthening communities. And the way we came about it—well, I'll just say that when I was incarcerated I had the idea of doing something called "Free Hearts," but I kept pushing it to the side. We started planning in 2015, but we didn't actually launch the organization until 2016. We knew that we wanted to do policy change, and we wanted to work on housing—there were millions of things we wanted to do—but we started off with a support group inside [the Nashville Women's Jail]. That little support group inside the jail was our first organizing space. Those were the first people we started organizing with, and then we just continued to build out from there.

Jack: How about you, Gicola?

Gicola Lane: I actually met Dawn for the first time in court. Our public defender's office was having a court watch program, and we had already launched participatory defense in 2016. I was doing that work, and it didn't really have an organizational home anymore. So I started out as a volunteer with Free Hearts, solely focused on participatory defense, and of course, the women that were meeting in the jail [in Nashville] naturally had cases for participatory defense. That's the angle that I came into Free Hearts with. From there, I became the state organizer. I would say that 2018 to 2019 is when we really started seeing the need to focus on building the organization statewide. So that's when we launched the Decriminalize Poverty campaign surveys and went all across the state talking to people who are most impacted by incarceration. Whereas originally, we had just been talking to Nashville folks, because we're both from here, so we always knew people who were cycling in and out of the jails. I would see old classmates in the jails, or classmates' siblings. And the same in the courthouse.

That's how we started building. Our organizing started with contacts that we already had, with people we already knew. At the time I was working at a local community center, and then I went on to go with the bail fund, and I started using that as a way to get folks out of jail. Then we found a pathway for me to come on staff at Free Hearts in 2019. So that was my journey.

Jack: How do you, as organizers, understand the role of the county jail in Tennessee? What do you see it being used for?

Dawn: The county jail is a site to warehouse bodies. As you know, the majority of people are there because they can't afford their bail—we have exorbitant bail amounts here. The jails also warehouse people for the state prison system. If you have like a six-year sentence or less, the state pays the county jail to incarcerate you. Jails also hold people—in

Davidson County, and I'll just say more generally—for ICE, and for the US Marshals.

I think of the jail as a site where families are broken, where housing is lost, where employment is lost—even with a short stay there. A site where families are broken up. It's a site where our community members—and a lot of our social problems—are disappeared from the community and from plain sight. But really, they do not disappear. They are just warehoused in the jail.

Gicola: The jail is a reminder of the harm and violence that our communities face. A lot of the things that we've heard from community members who are inside of our local jails are things that the majority of the public doesn't have a clue about. Which speaks to Dawn's point about disappearance. It also reminds me of just how disinvested we are from actually trying to build healthy, stable communities. We're throwing money in a place that we *know*—for years and for decades, centuries—has not helped our people who have landed up there. There's this narrative of rehabilitation and of the sheriffs being supportive and this, that, and the third, but at the end of the day a jail is a *horrible* place. I mean, it's horrible. It's dehumanizing. It's unhealthy in so many ways. From the environmental issues to the mental issues that it perpetuates, it is just a violent, nasty place. That's how I see it.

Jack: Can you talk about the Decriminalize Poverty campaign, how it came to be and the methods that you used, as well as the research that went into that campaign?

Gicola: One thing I remember is that when the Decriminalize Poverty campaign first started, we had been working on driver's license issues in Wilson County. When we were prepping and doing research about that, Dawn and I both looked at each other and were just like: "You know what? I lost my driver's license too." We talked about how normalized this was. And it shouldn't be normal—all this money that we didn't have at the time, just to pay to get our driver's licenses back, just this hole that you can end up in. We started connecting the dots as we were helping people navigate the same thing we had been through, and in doing so we were naming all the exploitative ways that the system takes monies from our families. That's something that even our families in participatory defense always talk about—how much the jail calls are going up, how much parking is when you're going to court, how bail is ridiculous, about electronic monitoring fees, this fee, that fee ... We were just like, "This is crazy. They're literally making billions off our families who are literally living below the poverty line." That's how it started.

We really wanted to put together a visual to help other people connect the dots the way we connected the dots, because a lot of people in our society are shamed. It's not *talked* about—how much legal debt people owe, or that you couldn't pay a ticket and then that ticket turned into another fee, and that's how you lost your driver's license. A lot of people just do not talk about these things. I think Free Hearts has really provided a space for people to feel comfortable talking about things like having fifty thousand dollars in court costs and restitution. Mouths drop when you say this, but this is a normal thing that's happening to people. So we put together a visual. It was just a little circle diagram showing how this all flowed together. It allowed us to have conversations all across the state. A lot of people could relate, and it resonated with people in terms of how ridiculous it is that this much money is being taken out of the pockets of the neediest people.

Dawn: Yeah, and I'll just add to that. When we were doing that driver's license work, we had just also finished finding plaintiffs for a lawsuit in Rutherford County for the private probation company there that was criminalizing poor people and sending them back to jail. And so to what Gicola said, we started realizing how all of these things—driver's license suspensions, private probation, money bail—were really connected. What was being touted as the alternative or as the solution for all of this was electronic monitoring. They were talking about it a lot in the legislature. People that were on the inside were like, "Well, you know, if I can get out of jail on a monitor, like, I will." But the thing is, it costs so much that if you can't afford to pay, then you have to go back.

When we were organizing in Rutherford County, we found thousands of plaintiffs that had been impacted by private probation. Even now, in some of the counties that we go into where we have participatory defense cases, we see almost full dockets of people who are locked up because they can't pay their probation, or people who basically have their bonds revoked because they can't pay their probation. It's all highly interconnected. There may be a bunch of different imposers and enforcers and mechanisms by which these court fees and other costs are imposed, but a family will experience the compounding effect of all of these things at once. A lot of times it leads people back to being incarcerated. We were starting to create that analysis around the criminalization of poverty. We were starting to see things that we needed to do, and that we really needed to build out, statewide.

But then there were still a lot of places in Tennessee where we were afraid to go, to be honest. We have a lot of, like, sundown towns here. But with the organizing around the Providence Community Corrections lawsuit we were afforded the opportunity to go into communities that historically we would not have been in. Places with Confederate flags and things like that. We realized from that experience that the level of poverty in some of these places was even worse than what we were accustomed to.

I remember on that campaign, one of the named plaintiffs on the lawsuit, they got a trailer with their lawsuit money. It ended up getting repossessed. And they had so many people living up in there, like everybody. Several family members came and lived in the trailer and then, you know, they didn't have the money to pay for the *full* thing yet, but they were waiting for the rest of the money. During that time, their trailer was repossessed.

I remember Cindy, Cindy Rodriguez, may she rest in peace. She was one of the named plaintiffs in the lawsuit. We used to have to go pick her up from different places. Whatever money she could come up with in the day, she would ask people if she could give them like $25 or something like that for her to live in there, to sleep in their shed for that night. I remember one of the times we went to pick her up, her arm was broken, and she said that the hospital had stopped taking her, because I guess she was never able to pay them. She was in so much pain, like, *so* much pain. She ended up dying like the next year.

These are people who were impacted by this compounding effect of not only this one thing that we were working with them about, the private probation, but also all of these other things that are interconnected and have a financial impact. People who were basically sent back to jail for not having money. Then on top of that they had all these other barriers: driver's license suspension, some had electronic monitors, other things as well. This really informed our analysis. The organizing around private probation gave us the opportunity to go to places and really start thinking about how to talk about all of this. That's when we started talking about, "Okay, this is the *criminalization of poverty*, and we need to decriminalize poverty." This is a way of understanding how we are connected across Tennessee, across the urban-rural divide. This is what's happening to poor, working-class people across our state. I think it was really good for us to kind of use that as a start, because that framing really was a door-opener and a conversation-starter and a dot-connector, and it pulled people out of isolation. Even in places where the culture is more "hush-hush" and where people are less accustomed to talking about being incarcerated and the impact that the system has on us. There is a lot of internalized shame. For us this analysis and framing around the criminalization of poverty was a way to kind of pull people out of that, to really be able to have some real conversations about how everything was interconnected.

Jack: Thank you. That is related to the next question I had, which is about how you actually organize against criminalization and incarceration in different parts of the state. Tennessee's such a big state, and it's a diverse state, and I was hoping you could talk about how you organize across the state. And I'm thinking about people who might be trying to do similar things, organizing across a diverse geography.

Gicola: One thing I always like to share about this is that we failed at it before we figured out what worked for us. I think that's really important to note. You know, Dawn, myself, and a few other people from the participatory defense work were going across the state and setting up shop and trying to have community dinners in places where people didn't know us. It was a very, very, very small few that would turn out for something like that. From there we developed the idea that we needed to invest in the leaders that already existed in these communities, which is the same thing we would want in our own communities. It was just that we didn't know anyone there. So we did outreach, online, to connect with directly impacted people in a multitude of ways and a multitude of campaigns.

One way we did this was through our fellowship. We've also met a lot of rural people through the *Free the Vote* campaign, which is a campaign to help people who have felony convictions get their voter rights restored in Tennessee. That has been very helpful. I always tell people: we failed before we got to the right experiment.

Dawn: Yeah, I totally agree. It was a trip. But you know, originally, what we did is we pulled out the map. And we just looked at the map. Now mind you, Tennessee is like three states in one. East Tennessee is like its own state and its own culture, more of an Appalachian culture. West Tennessee is more of a Delta culture, it's the Black Belt of the state and it has a feel of the Black Belt of the country as well. Middle Tennessee has its own flair. So when we first started the Decriminalize Poverty campaign, we had people in Nashville, which is where we were from, and which is where we started our organization. Then we had just done those two campaigns; one in Rutherford around the private probation, and then one in Wilson County around driver's license suspensions.

We knew some people in those three places basically, but we were looking at the full map, and our state is like a seven-hour drive from one side to the next. We basically used the map as the measurement of how we were doing with what we were doing. We had it broken down in judicial districts. Each week we would see how many people we had in the district and did we have people in any new districts. We just started knocking the map down like that. And Gicola's right. We absolutely did fail at the beginning by just thinking that we could go organize people's communities. But we were able, eventually, to find leaders and to give them the training that they needed to be able to organize. It was a sound investment in getting things up and going.

I think at the end, when we finished the survey, I think we had connected in seventeen of our thirty-one judicial districts. It was remarkable. And now we've connected with people in every single county from our work, and we are continuing to organize and continuing to grow. I will say that we've seen some crazy stuff. When we go into court in some of these counties, it seems like we've gone fifty years into the past, or more. I think that some of the time when we were popping up in people's communities, I think we probably were the talk of the town, but not the type of talk of the town we wanted to be, but more like: "Who are these people? Did y'all see them today, too? Yeah, I saw them today too." That type of thing.

Let me give the example of Weekly County, of what we have been able to do. Our trainer from there—Michelle Chapel—she was just such a great student when she went through her fellowship. She's very inquisitive and she's somebody that if she learns about one thing, she's going to go get like two books, read more about it, and she's going to watch the YouTube video. She's somebody that was just really into the training and has really applied herself and has kind of brought in people from some of the surrounding counties, and a lot of people know her in her own community. They know her from times that she was incarcerated and the struggles she went through early in her life, and it's still, like, held onto her in her small town. But I think what's really amazing is to see her take that reputation and the things that they knew her for—stuff that some people see shame in—but for her to be able to embrace the power of that. She's gotten a lot of remarks that, you know, "Wow, this is just so amazing that you're doing this work," I think it's really powerful to see what it looks like when somebody is trained and then able to just take the organizing work to their own community.

Jack: Gicola, did you want to say anything about that?

Gicola: Yeah. I think one of the major challenges—especially in the climate that we organize in today, is that a lot of people don't have the patience when you don't share the same ideology, and to really overcome that, and to not push a "you're wrong, and I'm right" sort of stance. I don't think that this situation is abnormal. I think that it's just that people don't normally talk to each other. It's very unlikely—unless you've lived in, or your family has connections to a rural place, that you would even go there. Like, we might not meet each other in everyday life, Jack. I think the biggest takeaway for me is that even though on paper we could be total opposites … Even in the example that Dawn shared, most people would never think, hell, *I* didn't think that Michelle would even be where she's at, and that was a learning experience for me, for all of us.

I've been trained a couple of times by an organizer named Carlos—he's based in Boston with the Anyi Institute. He used to always tell us, if you perfect your craft as an organizer, you should be able to organize anywhere. I think that kind of showed up here. One thing that I always hear about Free Hearts' work is that we don't come off as judgmental. That means not being judgmental as far as what you've been charged with or convicted with. But we've also worked on applying it to ideological differences in general and to political analysis. Just really understanding our state and what it's going to take to create change, to being at the legislature and understanding who really holds a lot of power in this state and understanding that the only way to change that is to deal with people all across the state who are facing very similar challenges and really being able to connect those dots.

I've seen it many, many times in organizing spaces where we discount folks when we don't agree, when we're not on the same political spectrum or that type of thing. But I think what really helped *us* was that mutual alignment on wanting and knowing that incarceration did not work for us. It did not work for our families and is not working for our communities. And what can we do together to change it?

We know that there's power in numbers. I really want to big up the political education and curriculum that Dawn put together for our fellows, because I think that helped open people's minds and started conversations that we never would have otherwise had. Like, we don't even have these conversations sometimes with our own families! I think just that open dialogue and debate—healthy debate and discussion —really allowed for people to open their minds to be willing to hear out others who come from very, very different backgrounds. People really did feel like they were getting something out of this, like it was beneficial for all of us, and it continues to be.

Jack: What would you tell people who are in a place where the county leaders are trying to build a new jail?

Dawn: Jails destroy communities. They destroy the environment. They destroy families. The people that they're going to be putting in there are your community members. In Tennessee, for example, we've lost so many hospitals. And some of those places where they've lost hospitals are places where they're wanting to put a jail or places where they don't have any other resources available. So I would tell people that really what the jail is going to do is disappear problems, but the problems will still be there. You will be better off using that money, or fighting to use that money, to build up the infrastructure that's really needed to keep the community safe—and to heal—as opposed to building a new jail, which we know is gonna be the site, and the cause, of much more destruction for the community.

Jack: What would you tell people who are in a small town or a small city who are trying to organize to fight jail expansion?

Gicola: I think what I would tell people is that it's all about just starting wherever makes sense for you. It doesn't have to be a formal organization. It doesn't have to be a big grand thing. You start with where you are and with the people who are around you. You know, we saw a lot of this for George Floyd. There were protests in places all across rural Tennessee that were four or five people here and there, holding posters up or standing outside of the county jails, things of that nature. People getting with other people who cared about something in their area. Even some of the people in East Tennessee who work with Free Hearts—they didn't know each other! It's crazy that Free Hearts introduced people in far East Tennessee who hadn't met each other before, who share similar backgrounds, who absolutely would not want the jail to be expanded.

Sometimes it's all about being able to just get with other people like that and to speak up—finding your folks in your own town and folks who are already having these conversations. Because they *are* already having these conversations. Whether it is on a large scale or not, the conversations are definitely happening, when you see a community that has been totally disinvested from, with all opportunities wiped out, they're *absolutely* talking about these things. A lot of Free Hearts staff members, our families come from rural Tennessee. A lot of us still have family members in rural Tennessee. So we know—from cousins and aunts and the whole nine— the reality of what they're facing. A lot of times, historical context, and intimidation, is keeping people from speaking up. We got comments like, "Nashville is not Chicago," when we first started to push back against the criminalization that was happening here. I think it's all about just speaking your truth, finding people that you align with who you can strategize with and who you can rely on, and you can feed each other's spirits. It can get heavy, and being able to find your community members who care and are passionate about these same issues and who are impacted by these issues is really important.

There are families all over this country and all over this world who are impacted by these issues. I think one of the most beautiful things that has come from our organizing is being able to create this space to talk about it. Because the moms, and the grandmas, they've *been* doing this. I have memories as early as from when I was a little girl of my grandmother driving all across the state visiting relatives in prisons. But sometimes it took years to even talk or connect to people who cared about this issue, or to even realize it's a systemic issue. You know, that's *my* story. Even with police violence, I didn't talk about what happened to my family for a long time. But then when I got older and I realized that it was a systemic issue and other families were going through this too, and that this wasn't an individualized thing. And that encouraged me. I think that also would be helpful for people who want to organize around this issue and who are disgusted by the way the money is being spent in their county and that so much is being heavily invested in incarceration. I think that those common denominators will absolutely help people come together to be able to forge whatever path they to need to create change.

Dawn: To end, I just want to bring up the importance of coalition building. I was thinking about one of our sister organizations in Alabama. They just had this jail fight, and they worked with a group that was very, very conservative, that was fighting the jail for a different reason—something about where the jail was going to be and how it was going to disrupt agriculture. They were an unlikely coalition. But these conservatives came together with these fierce abolitionists for this fight. I think sometimes it may be harder to think about coalition-building in a rural context, but there are always groups, whether they're formal, informal. Even in some of the places that we go to, they may not have a whole lot of activist infrastructure, but they have a whole lot of churches, a lot of faith homes. Figuring out how to build coalitions to fight the jail is important. As is rethinking the community infrastructure that you have, as it exists. There may be completely different reasons why people want to engage in the fight or in the struggle, but if we can work toward the same end, or if we can get them over to this side, then it still might be a good coalition to build.

7

Carceral Communities: Local Resistance to the Prison-Industrial Complex in the Mountain South

Amelia Kirby

Context

In the summer of 1998, I had come home from college and was visiting my family in Wise County, Virginia, where I grew up. Wise County is in the coalfields of Appalachia, in southwestern Virginia snug against the Kentucky border. My mother and I were driving down the Powell Valley, a wide open basin unfolding southwest from the lofts of the highest mountain in the county, buttressed by Wallens Ridge and Big Cherry Mountains to the south. The Powell Valley is exceptionally beautiful, and its beauty is precious because it's the one of the only places in Wise County that doesn't have mineable coal.

In the county as a whole, though, around 30 percent of the land is owned by absentee coal companies, and more than 40 percent, or well over 100,000 acres, has been destroyed by strip mining[1]. Mountaintop removal—a form of strip mining—involves the coal companies blasting hundreds of feet worth of soil, rock, plants, and animals off the tops of mountains to access the coal beneath. In Powell Valley, the geological

---

1 Austin Counts, "Fighting for Equitable Land Access in Southwest Virginia," *Front Porch Blog*, Appalachian Voices, December 11, 2020, appvoices.org.

protections from mining—the fact that the mountain has been left in place—meant that topping over the ridge and coming into the valley was always a breathtaking moment, no matter how many times I'd seen it.

But when I took a sharp breath as I drove into the valley with my mother that afternoon in 1998, it wasn't because of the beauty. Perched on Wallens Ridge, in the very center of that vast panorama, was what appeared to be a mountaintop removal strip job. I turned to my mother, wondering how there could be a strip mine going into this place that I had believed to be safe from that violation. She explained to me that it wasn't a mine but that it was site preparation for a prison.

That was the moment I learned about Wallens Ridge State Prison—a supermax that opened in April 1999 and has since been regarded as one of the most repressive and dangerous prisons in the country. Seeing that damaged mountainside in 1998 drew me into what has been a decades-long involvement in examining and addressing the implications of using imprisonment as an economic development strategy in the coalfields of Appalachia, including as co-director of a community media project that produced the documentary *Up the Ridge* (2006) and the radio program *Calls from Home*, which began in 2001. *Up the Ridge* examines the economic and human costs of rural prison-building through looking at the construction of Wallens Ridge. *Calls from Home*, hosted by media arts organization Appalshop's community radio station WMMT, broadcasts music and messages of love and support from families and loved ones on the outside into the eight prisons in the station's listening range.

In the last twenty-five years, Central Appalachia has had one of the highest concentrations of rural prison and jail expansion in the United States.[2] The proliferation of "cages in the

---

2 Sylvia Ryerson and Judah Schept, "Building Prisons in Appalachia: The Region Deserves Better," *Boston Review*, April 28, 2018, bostonreview.net.

coalfields" is closely linked to the decline of the coal industry and the rise of the opioid crisis.[3] Coal mining has experienced a massive decline in the last two decades. Eastern Kentucky lost 73 percent of its coal jobs between 2011 and 2018.[4] Concurrent with that decline has been the rise of the opioid epidemic. In the late 1990s, Purdue Pharma targeted Central Appalachia as an area with high levels of occupational pain from coal mining and commenced a juggernaut of misleading advertising and hard-press sales to doctors in the region, opening the gates to a profit-driven over-prescription of OxyContin and a devastating wave of addiction and death. Purdue Pharma's flooding of the coalfields with OxyContin, and the subsequent carceral response in the region, created two decades of an acute social crisis rooted not only in the fallout from widespread generational addiction but also in the criminalization of addiction. That fallout included the overdoses and deaths, the disruption of social and cultural institutions, and the destabilization of family structures as vast numbers of children are being raised by grandparents or other family members.[5] And while the pharmaceutical companies' executives receive slaps on the wrist, thousands of eastern Kentuckians suffering from substance use disorders have been arrested, convicted, and often incarcerated in new or expanded jails.

Leaders at the local, state, and federal levels have touted prisons and jails as a means of bringing in jobs and revenue to replace the jobs and revenue lost in the sharp decline of the coal industry. They have also touted police, prisons, and jails as a means of dealing with the opioid crisis. In a particularly symbolic act, many of the prisons—and at least one of the county

3 Judah Schept, *Coal, Cages, Crisis: The Rise of the Prison Economy in Central Appalachia* (New York: New York University Press, 2022).
4 Jack Norton and Judah Schept, "Keeping the Lights On: Incarcerating the Bluegrass," *In Our Backyards Stories*, March 4, 2019, vera.org.
5 Tarence Ray, "United in Rage: Half-Truths and Myths Propelled Kentucky's War on Opioids," *Baffler* 58 (July 2021), thebaffler.com.

jails—constructed in the region have been built on top of former strip mines with the assertion that this constitutes a productive and desirable use of the damaged landscape. And while there is widespread perception that there is significant long-term economic benefit in building prisons and jails, research indicates that rural communities that use prisons as economic development actually experience negative job growth.[6]

The story of prison jobs being touted as a solution to prop up the failing coal economy in Appalachia has been told extensively, but the use of county jails as an economic crutch for the region is an emerging aspect in the story of incarceration in Appalachia. In eastern Kentucky, there is incentive to turn to incarceration as an economic prop that goes beyond simply providing correctional or construction jobs. The system of coal severance taxes—wherein 4.5 percent of revenues from coal mined in each county are paid to the state and a percentage of that revenue is returned to the counties from which the coal is mined —has been in a precipitous decline, parallel to the coal industry, in the last decade. The loss of this tax revenue has put county governments in crisis, forcing the reduction or elimination of social services and occasioning a frantic scramble for alternative sources of revenue. This has in turn incentivized the use of county jails as overflow for—and a source of revenue from—the state department of corrections.[7]

Kentucky has over 24,000 state prisoners, but only around 12,000 state prison beds. Rather than seek to reduce the state prison population through sentencing reform, decriminalization, and release, Kentucky has opted to house nearly half of

---

6 Gregory Hooks et al., "Revisiting the Impact of Prison Building on Job Growth: Education, Incarceration, and County-Level Employment, 1976–2004," *Social Science Quarterly* 91, no. 1 (March 2010), 228–44; Robert Todd Perdue and Kenneth Sanchagrin, "Imprisoning Appalachia: The Socio-economic Impacts of Prison Development," *Journal of Appalachian Studies* 22, no. 2, pp. 210–33.

7 Norton and Schept, "Keeping the Lights On."

state inmates in county jails. The incentives for counties work like this: the Kentucky Department of Corrections spends approximately sixty-seven dollars per day for each person it locks up in a state prison. But it can pay counties around thirty-two dollars per day to lock up state-sentenced people, usually convicted of what are called Class D or Class C felonies (often drug-related convictions) in local jails. Because most county jails spend around twenty-five dollars per day for each incarcerated or detained person, there is about a ten-dollar-per-day incentive to house state prisoners in county beds.[8] These per diem payments add up, and they prop up local county budgets. They incentivize both jail crowding and the construction of bigger county jails, which are in turn filled with more people sentenced to Class D and C felonies, more people sentenced to misdemeanors, and more people held pre-trial, unable to pay bail. This approach encourages county and state elected officials to maintain high levels of local incarceration. Jails in eastern Kentucky stay full at an average of 140 percent of their rated capacity. Bell County in eastern Kentucky is at a whopping 224 percent.[9]

The monetary incentivization that encourages counties to rely on overcrowding their jails also leads to counties seeking to build bigger facilities with more beds to secure contracts with federal agencies. In Laurel County, in eastern Kentucky, the county government recently built a 1,000-bed jail with the express intention of renting beds to not only the state, but to the United States Marshals Service (USMS) and Immigration and Customs Enforcement (ICE). Laurel County has a population of around 58,000 people and yet has approximately one-third the number of beds of the entire New York City jail system.[10]

---

8 Ibid.

9 Jacob Kang-Brown, Chase Montagnet, and Jasmine Heiss, *People in Jail and Prison in 2020* (New York: Vera Institute of Justice, January 2021), vera.org.

10 Norton and Schept, "Keeping the Lights On."

This entrenches incarceration as a central component of the county's economy, despite clear research showing that such an approach does not produce positive economic outcomes.

Resistance

The challenges faced by people in Appalachia are daunting and significant—disinvestment, corporate control, environmental destruction, and mass incarceration. But there is also a rich and significant history of Appalachian resistance to oppression. The fierce battles of the United Mine Workers of America and the movement to win compensation for black lung have been central to defining national labor struggles. The anti-strip-mining movement and the grassroots organizing efforts to end the broad form deed are models of community-based environmental justice.[11] Appalachian activists and Deep South civil rights organizers have been collaborating on popular education at the Highlander Center in east Tennessee for over eighty years. The community media arts organization Appalshop and Harlan County's Higher Ground community-based theater project are both nationally lauded models of cultural organizing to address social injustices. And the work of the Letcher Governance Project (LGP) provides lessons from a nationally recognized grassroots effort to successfully resist the construction of a federal prison.

LGP was formed by people in Letcher County in response to a proposal to build a new federal prison in eastern Kentucky.

---

11 The broad form deed is a legal document that separates surface ownership of land from the ownership of the minerals beneath the surface. These deeds, most of which were put into place before the advent of strip mining, allowed companies to strip-mine land in eastern Kentucky without the permission of the landowner, destroying homes, cemeteries, and habitat with no recourse for the landowner. Its use in Kentucky was outlawed in 1988 by constitutional referendum following extensive citizen organizing.

While discussions about the prison began as early as 2005, the project accelerated in early 2016 with the congressional allocation of $444 million to the Bureau of Prisons to construct United States Penitentiary Letcher. Initially formed from a loose coalition of volunteers on the *Calls from Home* radio program on Appalshop's WMMT community radio, the group mounted a campaign to push for a re-visioning of what could be done in the region with the $444 million allocated for the prison.[12] They created an effective social media campaign with the hashtag #our444million, which framed the need for meaningful, community-controlled investment in the region, more transparency in the local democratic process, and the delegitimization of prisons as economic development. This campaign was met with retaliation from state and federal elected officials but was a key part of a movement that eventually led to the Federal Bureau of Prisons shelving the project in 2019.[13]

Foundation for Appalachian Kentucky

In late 2019, in a grant-making effort in part focused on the rise of rural incarceration, the Chan Zuckerberg Initiative (CZI) announced funding across multiple states and communities for projects to reduce mass incarceration. In eastern Kentucky, the Foundation for Appalachian Kentucky received a grant from CZI. The Foundation for Appalachian Kentucky (FAK) was well positioned to incorporate this work into their overall

12 *Calls from Home* is a radio program on WMMT that provides the opportunity for people with loved ones in any of the eight prisons in the listening area to call in and send messages directly to their loved one over the air. See Henry Gass, "'Calls from Home': How One Kentucky Radio Station Connects Inmates and Families," *Christian Science Monitor*, February 9, 2018, csmonitor.com.

13 Retaliation came in the form of implicit and explicit threats to funding of nonprofit and state-funded programs. Ryerson and Schept, "Building Prisons in Appalachia."

regional philanthropic strategy. Their model prioritizes com-munity capacity building and expanding financial resources for community-based solutions in the region. FAK's focus is on coalition building, economic transition, leadership devel-opment, and on creating a network of civic leaders actively engaged in change.

In 2020, FAK hired me to head what was initially intended to be a one-year project on criminal justice reform. As a com-munity foundation, FAK has been a strong voice in regional dialogues about the transition from a primarily coal-based economy to a robust and multipartite economy but had not previously included an analysis of the role of the carceral system in the Appalachian economy. Any sort of just economic transi-tion requires us to understand jails, prisons, and criminalization as part of the regional legacies of economic and environmental injustice. Because FAK earlier had not been directly involved in this kind of work, we started with internal popular education about the vast scope of the prison-industrial complex. That education covered such topics as systems of policing and state control, mass criminalization, mass incarceration, and mass surveillance, as well as the relationship between these systems and the economic and social Appalachian context.

Floyd County, Kentucky

FAK has a network of affiliated community foundations in twelve counties in and around southeastern Kentucky. The initial focus included building relationships with the foun-dation's affiliate boards with the long-term goal of shifting attitudes (i.e., hearts and minds) about the system of mass incarceration and our communities' reliance on it both for local revenue and for the management of regional poverty and inequality. In 2020 we launched a pilot program in Floyd County, Kentucky, in an effort to combine political education with a tangible, material grant-distribution process in order to demonstrate the feasibility of decarceration—and the feasibility of even working toward decarceration—in eastern Kentucky. Building on existing relationships with community members there, we established the Floyd County Re-Visioning Team, comprised of members of the affiliate board, FAK staff, and people from around Floyd County who are concerned with issues related to the criminal legal system.

At the outset we agreed upon a set of values and goals for our work together, which were in part an effort to interweave abolitionist values in the process while maintaining space for community self-determination. They are as follows:

We believe:
- Mass incarceration is harmful to our community and our economy.
- A healthy fiscal outlook for Floyd County should not be reliant on carceral systems.
- Prevention is an economic engine as well as an engine of health and safety. Prevention from involvement with the justice system brings both prosperity and wellness.
- Community safety and security can be realized when everyone in Floyd County has what they need for safe, healthy, and stable lives.

Floyd County is a rural mountain county in the eastern Kentucky coalfields. The Floyd County jail (officially called the Floyd County Detention Center) is in Prestonsburg, the county seat. The jail is generally full and stays at about 140 percent of its rated capacity. Between 1985 and 2018, the jail incarceration rate in Floyd County rose 630 percent. During this same period, the jail incarceration rate for women in the county rose nearly 7,000 percent.

The Re-Visioning Team's initial grantmaking focused on getting resources to people in the Floyd County jail. In collaboration with a local behavioral health agency and a regional legal services agency, we began to work directly with people in the Floyd County jail and established two paid positions toward that end. A resource coordinator was tasked with facilitating support for people in jail as they prepare to get out and re-enter the community. This support includes helping people obtain official documentation (birth certificate, driver's license, photo ID, etc.) and assisting with Social Security benefits, health care, veterans' benefits, Medicare, Medicaid, employment, housing, legal assistance, and other community resources. We designed a legal service position to help with the civil legal needs of people in the county jail, including expungement, public benefits, divorce, fines and fees, and consumer bankruptcy. The person working in this position also helps with community legal education and outreach and works with community groups to strengthen understanding and capacity around reentry needs. Within six months, the two positions had served over 1,000 people.

Lessons and Next Steps

As this work develops, and as I have continued to work through the ongoing contradictions between my own abolitionist commitments and the formal structure of the foundation in which I work, I continue to reflect on best practices—on what works to get people out of jail, and to stop the construction of new prisons and jails. We are learning as we go. Mass incarceration is in many ways a local issue. This is especially true in eastern Kentucky, where the federal government is trying to site a new prison, and where the state government both builds state prisons *and* moves much of the functioning of the state prison system to the county jails. Organizing against incarceration means having many small conversations and connections. It also means learning from those already doing the work and learning with those who are engaging with the issues for the first time. It means taking advantage of what you've got available in the moment, and understanding that an imperfect vessel may still advance the overall work. The bail fund, in addition to getting people out of jail, creates a context for people to consider the absurdity of money bail. It helps expand the number of people in Floyd County who are actively reckoning with how damaging bail is, and by extension, makes it more likely that they will critically engage with other ways the system is causing harm.

My work now is aimed toward creating the conditions for this kind of analysis and resistance—for seeding the ground for questioning what we've been told is the only and best option for the future of our communities. Or to borrow the words of theorist allies, to cultivate the creation of an abolitionist geography by developing nodes of resistance.[14] These nodes, or pockets, or as we might consider it in the mountains, these emerging hollers of resistance are threaded throughout Appalachia, and it is an ongoing project to interweave them into an ever-stronger whole.

I grew up hearing people in my family sing a song called *Hard Times in the Wise County Jail*.[15] It was written in 1928 by a man named Dock Boggs. Wise County was one of the first places in the central Appalachian mountains where coal was mined by corporations. It is a place that colonial, capitalist, and carceral forces have been intertwined and operating for centuries. My

---

14 I learned this phrase from Judah Schept as we were discussing the work in eastern Kentucky on a drive up Interstate 75 on the Kentucky/Tennessee border while returning from a conference in Chattanooga. I am indebted to Schept for this framing and for his articulation and analysis of the relationship between coal and imprisonment.

15 *The officers around Norton/Are a dirty old crew*
They will arrest a poor man/And look him plumb through
His pockets they'll pick/And his clothes they'll sell
For twenty-five cents/They would send him to hell
It's hard times in the Wise County jail
It's hard times I know

family's relationship to this song was in part related to the risks they were running as environmental justice activists. They were watching the places they loved get dynamited, and they were formulating legal and extralegal answers to that destruction. They were worried about going to jail, but they were more worried about the future of the place they loved.

Since I started writing this piece, the Federal Bureau of Prisons has announced it is reactivating the plan to build a prison on an abandoned strip mine in Letcher County, Kentucky. As we are formulating a second round of resistance to this abysmal proposal, I am hopeful that the interwoven network of communities and individuals we have been building with for the last three years will have a strong voice and clear sense of agency in the fight to reject imprisonment as the future of our home.

8

Communities Over Cages— the (Ongoing) Campaign to Close the Atlanta City Jail

Xochitl Bervera and Wes Ware

With deep gratitude to Marilynn Winn and Robyn Hasan of Women on the Rise and the powerful organizations making up the Communities Over Cages Campaign Alliance[1]

The Communities Over Cages Campaign launched in 2018 to close the Atlanta City Detention Center (ACDC), a 1,100-bed jail that dominates the downtown skyline. The campaign sought to end the use of the building as a jail, transform it into a Center for Wellness and Freedom, and reinvest millions of dollars back into the communities most harmed by mass incarceration. This campaign was built on years of organizing

1 The Communities Over Cages: Close the Jail ATL Campaign Anchor Team includes Southern Center for Human Rights, Georgia Latino Alliance for Human Rights, Legal Action Center, Black Futurists Group, Georgia Coalition Against Domestic Violence, Showing Up for Racial Justice, Policing Alternatives and Diversion Initiative and the ACLU Georgia. The broader Alliance includes more than fifty organizations in support of the campaign, which can be found at closethejailatl. org. Authors would also like to give special thanks to Che Johnson-Long. For more on this campaign, see Che Johnson-Long, "Starving the Beast: Practical Abolition in Atlanta," *National Law Review Journal* 77, no. 2 (2020): 57–80.

to shift policymakers away from carceral approaches to public health, and a chance for city leaders to move money away from institutions that harm Atlanta's Black community and into community-based programs. Led by the Black, formerly incarcerated women of Women on the Rise and their parent organization, the Racial Justice Action Center, the five-year-long campaign celebrated many victories and mourned just as many defeats.

While there are many subplots to the story of this campaign, what follows is our best attempt to pull lessons learned in hopes it might be useful to other abolitionist organizers. Perhaps the most salient lesson follows from the fact that as this piece goes to press, the building is still being used to cage people, despite promises that it will close as a jail "very soon." Of course, the criminal justice system is highly resilient and will continually find ways to stay alive. Abolitionist campaigns to close jails and prisons, defund the police, or otherwise shrink the punitive legal system will always be extremely difficult, facing long odds and ferocious, wily, determined opposition. As such, abolitionist campaigns require building real and lasting power in our communities in the form of organizations or formations that can persist, adapt, and seize political opportunities while remaining true to abolitionist principles and vision. The opposition will, in turn, adapt, persist, and counterattack. The Communities Over Cages Campaign is a campaign that was won. Then lost. Then won and lost again. The battle continues.

Building the Beast

In 1990, the International Olympic Committee chose Atlanta to host the Centennial Olympic Games. Almost immediately, Atlanta's City Council passed a series of "quality of life," or "broken windows," ordinances authorizing the targeting of low-level offenses. Nearly 100 percent of city ordinance arrests were of visibly poor Black people, sent to an already overcrowded county jail.[2]

In early 1995, one year before the Olympics, city leaders announced the completion of its first Olympic project (before a single sporting venue was complete): a shiny new jail, standing seventeen stories high in the heart of downtown Atlanta.[3] Over the next two decades, the availability of beds in ACDC distorted nearly every public health and safety policy, making arrest and detention the default "solution" to houselessness, mental health crises, domestic violence, and substance use. It also supersized the power of Atlanta police to exert their authority over predominantly poor and Black neighborhoods.

Starving the Beast: Abolitionist Organizing Emerges

In 2012, the Racial Justice Action Center and its two projects, Solutions Not Punishment Collaborative and Women on the Rise, began confronting criminalization, seeking not to reform but to remake the city's public safety system. Building on previous community activism[4], this explicitly abolitionist organizing foregrounded an intersectional analysis and brought together various groups targeted by Atlanta's carceral state: Black and Brown, queer, trans and gender nonconforming people, immigrants, formerly incarcerated women, sex workers, and others.

2 It's worth noting that this was not the first time Atlanta created crimes to control Black and poor people's movement and presence. After the Civil War, Atlanta's Pig Laws made it basically illegal for free Black people to be on the streets of the city without being able to show the "papers" of an active work contract; laws which often effectively forced formerly enslaved people back to the plantations they had just escaped.

3 Research Action, *The History of the Atlanta City Detention Center* (December 2018), PDF available at lac.org.

4 In particular, authors would like to acknowledge organizations like Building Locally to Organize for Community Safety (BLOCS) and informal groups that organized for justice for Kathryn Johnston.

This coalition cut its teeth on campaigns that made modest but significant policy changes. We "banned the box" on city employment applications, repealed over forty "criminal" ordinances from the city code and decriminalized possession of marijuana. We won a campaign to create what is now the Atlanta/Fulton County Policing Alternatives and Diversion Initiative (PAD), using harm reduction principles to stop arrests and provide real services. At the same time, Women on the Rise, alongside the Southern Center for Human Rights and Southerners on New Ground, organized against cash bail. In February 2018, cash bail was ended for several city ordinance violations.[5]

Before long, the average nightly population at ACDC dropped from between 700 and 600 to around 400 and 200 per night. [6]

The Launch of the Communities Over Cages: Close the Jail ATL Campaign

In the spring of 2018, the Communities Over Cages: Close the Jail ATL Campaign was officially launched. The Atlanta City Detention Center sucked $32.6 million dollars each year out of the city's budget in the name of "public safety" and caused immense suffering for the poorest of our city's residents and immigrant families.[7] With a true diversion program finally in place, we knew it was time to force the city to divest from the jail altogether and invest in our communities.

Ms. Marilynn Winn, Co-Founder and then Director of Women on the Rise was the first to suggest that we were ready to launch this campaign. As organizers, we understood that

---

5 "Mayor Keisha Lance Bottoms Signs Cash Bond Ordinance into Law," City of Atlanta, February 6, 2018, atlantaga.gov.

6 Amy Cross et al., *Close the Atlanta City Detention Center and Deliver Long-Term Public Safety* (New York: Vera Institute of Justice, February 2021), vera.org.

7 Research Action, *History of the Atlanta City Detention Center.*

this campaign was substantively different from our previous fights. The jail had a lucrative federal contract in place that would need breaking. The Atlanta Police Department was still accustomed to arresting people for the most minor ordinance violations and it was easier and faster to book people at ACDC than at the County Jail. Bail bonds, food service, and commissary companies all benefited from contracts at the jail. There were over 200 employees who relied on the jail for their jobs. Further, there was a locally grown, charismatic Chief Jailer Patrick Labat—a friend of many elected officials who endeared himself to others by using "voluntary inmate labor" to clean up the city's neighborhoods at no cost to them.

Our previous campaigns had been powerful, often to repeal or reform laws, and they had certainly encountered ideological opposition. But like most municipal jails, ACDC was its own small empire, with multiple stakeholders benefiting from its continued operation. We knew campaigning to close down the jail would provoke a response from these self-interested stakeholders, requiring that we pivot at every turn. Were we ready? We were as ready as we were going to be.

For six months, organizers put our heads down and engaged our fundamental campaign strategies. We built a broad-based alliance of more than fifty organizational members, spanning issues of immigrant rights, housing, HIV, LGBTQ issues, and reproductive justice. We built our own base through community outreach, specifically looking for our folks who had been inside the jail. We identified and educated elected official campaign "champions" who could move the reform through the policy process. We educated the larger public through research materials, presentations, social media, and press conferences. We collected and distributed our members' stories of lives disrupted by the jail. We had hard conversations with the jail's employees and released policy briefs that called on the city to ensure the workers got a "lift up, not a layoff." We exposed the fiscal absurdity of the facility that it cost the city more to hold people inside ACDC than it would put them up in some of Atlanta's fanciest hotels.

Abolish ICE: A Window of Opportunity and an Early Victory

One of the biggest opportunities of the campaign was the potential to unite different communities targeted for jailing. ACDC was divided into what insiders called the "city side" and the "immigration side." In 2012, the city contracted with ICE to detain immigrants in the jail.[8] By 2018, ACDC had a daily population of around 150 people on municipal offenses on the "city side" and close to 300 immigrants on "the immigration side." This provided an organizing opportunity to unite criminal justice and immigrant justice organizations and toward the closure of ACDC.

However, this organizing opportunity also posed a campaign challenge. Ending a contract between a municipality and a federal agency that brings millions into the city is not an easy task. As one of the campaign's earliest actions, Project South and Georgia Detention Watch released a report highlighting the inhumane treatment of the immigrant detainees in ACDC.[9] Together with other groups like the Georgia Latino Alliance for Human Rights and Black Alliance for a Just Immigration, we rallied at the jail and packed city hall to highlight the issue and demand the city take action. While we gained little ground in ending the contract that day, we laid vital groundwork for further organizing.

Organizing opportunities can come from the strangest of places. In 2018, Trump's Department of Justice (DOJ)

---

8 Priyanka Bhatt et al., *Inside Atlanta's Immigrant Cages* (Project South and Georgia Detention Watch, August 2018), projectsouth.org; Research Action, *History of the Atlanta City Detention Center*.

9 Bhatt et al., *Inside Atlanta's Immigrant Cages*.

announced its implementation of the "zero tolerance" policy at the border.[10] Media coverage of immigrant families separated and children held in cages sparked outrage and protests in Atlanta. Thousands of Black, Brown, and white Atlantans chanted "No More Cages" in the streets and joined calls to end horrific immigration policies. Organizers made the connection between border family separation and the separation and destruction of families through the criminal legal system. Our communities had reached a new level of understanding that humans of any age shouldn't be locked in cages and that white supremacy was fueling these injustices.

Atlanta's predominantly Black Democrat elected officials, including newly elected Mayor Keisha Lance Bottoms, were moved by protests against this egregious border policy. Mayor Bottoms ended the city's detention contract with ICE in May of 2018, stating that, "Atlanta will no longer be complicit in a policy that intentionally inflicts misery on a vulnerable population without giving any thought to the horrific fallout."[11]

This was a vital victory for the Communities Over Cages Campaign. It swiftly removed the then-largest population of people in the jail and simultaneously ended one of the largest financial interests in its operation. As a campaign, we felt like we were on a roll.

Building a Champion

One of the most important aspects of building campaigns is to find the right champion—the elected official who will work with your organization and membership base to facilitate

---

10 "Family Separation—A Timeline," Southern Poverty Law Center, March 23, 2022, splcenter.org.

11 Jeremy Redmond, "Atlanta Calls for ICE to Move Its Detainees Out of the City Jail," *Atlanta Journal-Constitution*, September 6, 2018, ajc.com.

your demands becoming policy. We knew our best choice for a champion was the newly elected Mayor Bottoms whose late father had been incarcerated when she was a girl.

After months of meeting with her staff, the campaign won an audience with her in January of 2019. In that meeting, she assigned her staff to work with us on the first piece of legislation needed to create a design team process. This step was a way to both guarantee broad community involvement and generate buy-in from decision-makers. At the meeting's conclusion, she posed with the group holding up the "Close the Jail ATL" T-shirt we had brought for her.

Yet, during the campaign, our relationship with Mayor Bottoms changed like the weather: sometimes warm, often heated, then increasingly cold. On national media, Mayor Bottoms spoke passionately about closing ACDC and turning the building into a "Center for Equity." However, she kept the campaign's leaders at arms' length, frequently communicating with organizers through go-betweens.

Building a Design Team

In the spring of 2019, we proposed and won our design team legislation. Mayor Bottoms went on the news and declared that Atlanta would "no longer be in the jail business" and that she planned to close the city jail.[12] While organizers celebrated that night, we also knew that it was just the beginning.

The Reimagining Atlanta City Detention Center Taskforce partnered with abolitionist architects at Designing Justice, Designing Spaces to create an innovative community-driven design process. We surveyed Atlantans about which design people liked best and released a report, "Raze & Replace," to

---

12 "Mayor Keisha Lance Bottoms' Legislation"; "Mayor Bottoms Says Atlanta Is Out of the Jail Business," *Atlanta Daily World*, May 22, 2019, atlantadailyworld.com.

push for design options that demolished the jail. But then the trouble began. With the COVID-19 pandemic as the convenient excuse, collaborative planning meetings with the mayor's office ended—effectively pushing the community out of the process.

Even more concerning, Mayor Bottoms' actions started to feel like political theater. In one instance, Mayor Bottoms made a public declaration that she was removing $12.5 million from the Atlanta Department of Corrections (ADOC). What she did not say was that the line item was simply shifted to a new "department" that simply replicated the ADOC's functions.[13]

Knowing the status quo's most effective tactic is to stall, we focused on securing a specific closure date for ACDC. As Mayor Bottoms dragged her feet, space for opposition grew. A right-wing failed mayoral candidate, who later won a seat on city council, Mary Norwood, began opposing the project, mobilizing wealthy, white residents in Buckhead (an area north of the city long known for its attempts to form their own majority white city). At the same time, the media began fear-mongering about rising crime.

Defund the Police: Another Window of Opportunity

Less than a month after the police murder of George Floyd and uprisings across the country, an APD officer shot and killed twenty-seven-year-old Rayshard Brooks in Atlanta, making plain that racism and police violence was as much a problem in our city as in Minneapolis.[14] Protestors filled the streets echoing the Black Lives Matter movement's demands to defund the police.

---

13 Office of Budget and Fiscal Policy, *City of Atlanta Fiscal Year 2022 Proposed Budget* (2021), atlantaga.gov.

14 "What to Know about the Death of Rayshard Brooks," *New York Times*, November 21, 2022, nytimes.com.

In this same time period, Mayor Bottoms released her proposal for the next year's budget, which included $18 million for jail operations—not a cent decrease from the year before.[15] Organizers realized she had no intention of closing it within the year. Making connections between defunding the police and defunding the Atlanta Department of Corrections, we joined forces and demanded both departments' budgets be slashed. Despite protests and sixteen hours of public comment to reduce funding to the police and ADOC, the Council, with support from the mayor, appallingly *increased* APD's budget.[16]

Then in the final blow of 2020, our staunchest opponent, ACDC Chief Jailer Patrick Labat, was elected Sheriff of Fulton County.[17] Fulton County encompasses Atlanta and several other municipalities. For over a decade, the chronically overcrowded Fulton County Jail had been searching for ways to expand. As ACDC emptied, Fulton County officials started to eye the building as potential county jail beds.

Labat's first act in office was asking the mayor for ACDC to be turned over to the County to expand his jail empire.[18] His request co-opted messages of "racial justice" through rhetoric about his commitment to alleviating the overcrowding crisis at the Fulton County Jail. We had foreseen that Fulton County might try to take over ACDC and warned the mayor's office of this possibility six months earlier. Yet by dragging their feet on closing the jail, they had opened the door for this to occur.

While the mayor had the political power to block Fulton County from turning the ACDC building into an annex of the

---

15 Office of Budget and Fiscal Policy, *City of Atlanta Fiscal Year 2021 Proposed Budget.*

16 Maggie Lee, "Atlanta City Council Approves Budget. It Does Not Defund the Police," *Saporta Report,* June 22, 2020, saportareport.com.

17 Martel Sharpe, "Patrick Labat Wins Fulton County Sheriff Runoff," *Atlanta Voice,* August 12, 2020, theatlantavoice.com.

18 Everett Catts, "Fulton Sheriff's Push to Buy Atlanta City Detention Center Continues Debate over Its Use," *Neighbor,* January 13, 2021, mdjonline.com.

county jail, she did not have the political power to secure the financing to turn the building into something else. Her support for closing the jail and turning it into a "Center for Equity" became less of a commitment and more of a talking point in the wake of the George Floyd uprisings.

Victory Unraveling

In May of 2021, Mayor Bottoms announced she would not run for reelection despite holding more than seventy percent favorable rating from residents. As our most powerful champion and the only person blocking the county from taking over the jail, her announcement was devastating. Mayor Bottoms leaving office diminished the power of the Close the Jail ATL campaign.[19]

It became clear that if the building remained standing without Mayor Bottoms to block a takeover, Fulton County would find a way to revive the building as a jail. We realized we needed to collectively map out a new strategy. If we were going to defend the wins to date and see the jail's closure, we would have to get involved in local elections like never before.

To build power, we decided to inject the jail into election discourse, make the issue of "divest/invest" a key campaign issue, and force candidates into recognizing both our political power and how popular closing the jail was. We decided to borrow from our opponents the tactic of polling voters to gain data and devise a persuasive ad campaign based on the arguments that voters found most compelling for closing the jail.

The results of the poll showed that a super majority of voters supported the jail's closure and would be more likely to support a mayoral candidate who was willing to close the Atlanta City

---

19 Jaclyn Diaz and Scott Neuman, "Atlanta Mayor Cites Triumphs, Disappointments in Decision Not to Run for Reelection," npr.org, May 7, 2021.

Detention Center.[20] Equipped with this information, Women on the Rise and Working Families Party created an ad that ran for several weeks at prime time on local stations calling on community members to contact city council to demand the jail's immediate closure.[21]

The ads worked. Closing and repurposing the jail made an appearance at several mayoral and city council debates and forums. Candidates were forced to answer hard questions and our framing was taken up by several of the most progressive candidates. Women on the Rise worked with allies such as the Georgia Latino Alliance for Human Rights, Working Families Party, and Showing Up for Racial Justice to knock on thousands of doors to educate voters on the candidates and the issue of the jail's closure. Hundreds of people put Close The Jail signs in their yards. We met with as many candidates as we could to educate them about ACDC, co-sponsored forums and encouraged them to take pledges to see our work through if they were elected.

Simultaneously, the Policing Alternatives and Diversion Initiative was working on a "Hail Mary" strategy to block a county takeover of the jail. They worked out a collaboration between the city and the county to create a 24/7 Diversion Center to be located on the ground floor of ACDC. By starting the process of converting the building into a place where people can get services and not sentences, PAD ushered in community services and also created what could hopefully become an effective block to jail expansion in the same building. The fall 2021 election appeared to be a victory for the campaign. Two longtime tough-on-crime council members lost their seats to

---

20 HIT Strategies, *Closing ACDC—A Progressive Path to Public Safety in Atlanta: Poll Results July 2021* (September 2021), closethe jailatl.org.

21 Communities Over Cages: Close the Jail ATL, "Bold Ad Campaign Tackles Public Safety: Urges Action to Close and Repurpose the Extra City Jail," closethejailatl.org.

progressive supporters of our campaign. The new mayor, Andre Dickens, had sponsored the legislation to create the Task Force to Reimagine ACDC while on City Council. We were hopeful that Mayor Dickens might carry forward our vision for closing and perhaps even demolishing the jail.

But in a stunning betrayal, Mayor Dickens went back on his word. In August 2022, Dickens teamed up with Sheriff Patrick Labat to introduce surprise legislation to lease 700 jail beds to the county for the next four years.[22]

Over five years, we had been able to block the Fulton County Jail lease, transforming what could have been an easy and crushing defeat into opportunities to fight another day. Through our committed organizing, we had become seen as experts in decarceration and safety. The relationships we had developed across all levels of government, media, and Atlanta communities meant the lease issue was not just quietly accepted. But after two years of being in a defensive posture, we were unable to create enough momentum to defeat Mayor Dickens's legislation. Despite overwhelming resident support to close the jail, and multi-stakeholder review boards and expert reports in favor of closure,[23] City Council approved the legislation by ten votes to four.[24] Even some of our previous jail closure champions chose

---

22 Kristen Holloway, "City of Atlanta Proposes Temporary Lease of Its Jail Space to Fulton County to Prevent Overcrowding," WSB-TV, August 2, 2022, wsbtv.com.

23 Legal Actions Center, *Fiscal Analysis of Proposed Lease of Atlanta City Detention Center to Fulton County* (2022), lac.org; Center for Innovations in Community Safety, *Reducing Jail Overcrowding Without Increasing Crime* (Georgetown Law, 2022), law.georgetown.edu; ACLU, *There Are Better Solutions: An Analysis of Fulton County's Jail Population Data* (2022), aclu.org; Justice Policy Board, *Fulton County Jail Population Review: Assessing Short- and Long-Term Jail Use Trends* (November 18, 2022).

24 "City Council Votes to Lease Old Atlanta City Detention Center to County Inmates," 11Alive, August 17, 2022, 11alive.com; J. D. Capelouto, "In Contentious Meeting Atlanta City Council OKs Leasing

the new mayor, the sheriff, old "lock 'em up" legacies, and their political careers over the will of the people and the possibility of a transformed Atlanta.

In December 2022, all 350 women held in Fulton County Jail were transferred with hundreds more incarcerated men on their way to be caged in the once-about-to-be-shuttered Atlanta City Detention Center.[25]

Impact and Lessons Learned

Because of this campaign and the work of its many coalition partners, we have made real, significant gains in Atlanta toward abolition.

Hundreds fewer people suffer behind bars on any given night in Atlanta, adding up to thousands fewer incarcerations every year. The city no longer partners with ICE to detain immigrants in this or any other locally controlled facility. The campaign (and its predecessors) drew powerful attention to and curtailed the use of police to handle "offenses" that are fundamentally about poverty, houselessness, and substance use. Thousands of Atlantans were involved in a truly participatory planning process that envisioned the transformation of a facility built to cage and punish into one that could serve our multifaceted communities.

And yet, the building is still in use as a jail. While an entire floor has been renovated for use as a diversion center, it is not closed. It is not a Center for Wellness and Freedom. It is not the story of victory that we wish it was. However, the story of this divest-and-dismantle campaign holds many lessons for

Jail Beds to Fulton County," *Atlanta Journal-Constitution*, August 16, 2022, ajc.com.

25 Miles Montgomery, "350 Female Detainees Transferred to Atlanta Detention Center from Union City," Atlanta News First, December 17, 2022, atlantanewsfirst.com.

those who seek to dismantle carceral institutions and facilities in our cities and counties.

One is that it is hard—*very hard*—to close a jail. It involves going up against a very powerful carceral state that has tentacles expanding into nearly every aspect of our cities, including vested financial interests in contracts from incarceration. It involves multiple abolitionist reform measures, like decriminalizing offenses, ending cash bail, ending contracts with ICE and other carceral players, and creating disincentives for locking more people up. But even that is not enough to stop a carceral state in its tracks. We must also be strategic thinkers, take advantage of small windows of opportunity, create savvy messaging, engage directly with elected officials through insider/outsider maneuvering, flank champions while holding them accountable, and make a way through for our organizing targets.

If there is any single lesson to be learned, it is that true grassroots organizing—knocking on doors, educating and empowering our communities, mobilizing and engaging, and staying close to the people—remains the most powerful tool we have. While we will sometimes move from being on the offensive to being on the defensive, and while our successes, if substantial, bring backlash and serious political opposition, we can and will weather the storms if we stay grounded in the people who are the power behind everything we do.

9

Federal Courts, FEMA Dollars, and Local Elections in the Struggle Against Phase III in New Orleans

An Interview with Lexi Peterson-Burge of Orleans Parish Prison Reform Coalition

Lydia Pelot-Hobbs: To start us off, could you explain a little bit about the fight around "Phase III" of the Orleans Parish Prison/Orleans Justice Complex?

Lexi Peterson-Burge: When Hurricane Katrina hit New Orleans, it demolished much of the previous jail complex, which was called Orleans Parish Prison but was commonly referred to as OPP. On any given day pre-Katrina, OPP was housing six thousand five hundred incarcerated folks. It was one of the largest county or parish jails in the United States. In many ways it operated and functioned as a prison, with the number of state prisoners locked up there more than a county or parish jail. When Katrina happened, the floods demolished the complex and thousands and thousands of incarcerated folks were left to drown, for dead.[1] It was horrific.

---

1 As detailed in the ACLU National Prison Project's report *Abandoned and Abused*, the New Orleans city government made the decision not to evacuate OPP when a mandatory evacuation was called for the city in the days before Hurricane Katrina. Instead, other parishes' jails (including juvenile detention facilities) were evacuated to OPP, leading to the jail being filled over capacity when the levees broke. Jail staff abandoned their posts, and incarcerated people at OPP were left to the

And when reconstruction started after Katrina, there was a large fight around what this new Orleans Parish jail complex would look like. The sheriff at that time, Marlin Gusman, wanted to use the federal funds coming from FEMA to build a large jail complex with multiple phases. This is what he called each building: Phase I, and Phase II. Phase I is the kitchen and warehouse space for the jail, which advocates critiqued was built large enough for a jail with over eight thousand beds. Phase II is the main jail building that is now known as OJC or the Orleans Justice Center. But if you look at the pictures of how the OJC is set up, there is this big gap in between the buildings of Phase I and Phase II, with a bridge that goes nowhere. It doesn't connect to anything. Gusman's original plan was to build Phase III in that open space. Phase III was originally supposed to be an additional maximum-security housing unit.

But the Orleans Parish Prison Reform Coalition (OPPRC) started to fight against Gusman's plan to rebuild the jail complex as large as it was previously. After several years of community organizing, the city council was convinced to put a cap on the number of beds the new jail complex would be built, to 1,438 in 2011. This was a huge win.

Around the same time there was advocacy around getting a consent decree on the jail. In 2012, federal judges placed a federal consent decree stating that the living conditions were horrendous, there was no support for incarcerated folks who are dealing with mental health issues, and that those people needed to be housed differently than the other incarcerated folks who were not deemed to have mental health diagnoses or who were not in behavioral health crisis. So when the consent decree was put on the sheriff's

---

floodwaters for days. Many people survived only through the solidarity of other prisoners saving their lives. See National Prison Project of the ACLU, *Abandoned and Abused: Orleans Parish Prisoners in the Wake of Hurricane Katrina* (Washington, DC: ACLU, 2006), aclu.org.

office, the Phase III endeavor turned from the original plan to build this maximum-security building in the gap between the other buildings, to Phase III is going to be where we house our folks who have mental health diagnoses or who are currently experiencing behavioral health crisis. Phase III was redesigned really to be a mental health institution, but it is really a jail. It was originally supposed to be one hundred sixty-four additional "mental health" beds, one hundred six "medical beds," and two hundred fifty-six "re-entry beds." Following activists' outrage at this proposal, it was brought down to eighty-nine mental health beds with a specific tailoring for folks who might be in a mental health crisis or have a mental health diagnosis: special doors, special windows, special beds that were created to limit the ability for someone to possibly cause harm to themselves. A circular floor plan, so that a person sitting in the middle could see all the cells.

They were just missing the beat completely. The thought process that folks experiencing mental health crises would need to go to jail to access mental health support felt off. But the argument from the sheriff's office was, we don't provide adequate care for those who are incarcerated with these kind of diagnoses or crises. So if we build it, we will be able to provide those folks with that "adequate care" and be able to come into compliance with the consent decree. So that's a little back history about Phase III.

Lydia: This also makes me think about the signs around New Orleans recently to encourage people to vote for a new jail tax that said "OPSO [Orleans Parish Sheriff's Office] Cares," and about how widespread this articulation of care has been around jailing.

Lexi: Yeah, even with the new sheriff administration—which I was in support of from my understanding that abolition doesn't happen overnight, and we needed to get Gusman out of office—the emphasis is on trying to change the narrative of jail itself, as a place where people can come and receive care or support. It's a very interesting manipulation of folks' perceptions of what is actually happening behind those jail walls. That we would say, "Let's use FEMA funding that is supposed to support and help the recovery and reconstruction of our city post-Katrina to build a psychiatric prison. That is where our people are going to receive the best care."

Lydia: Can you tell me about how and when the Phase III fight started to ramp up? What were those dynamics like?

Lexi: I moved to New Orleans in November of 2020, at the height of the pandemic. I got involved with OPPRC and came on at the beginning of 2021 as OPPRC's deputy director. I joined this fight that had been happening for almost a decade prior to me being here. I think that's important to say. But we noticed in 2021 a very large ramp-up in the fight because a few things were happening.

The pandemic was at its height, and the jail population was at the lowest it had been in decades. The thought of expanding the jail and building additional beds past that 1,438-bed cap that was passed post-Katrina felt regressive. Community advocates, including the folks who had been organizing in OPPRC for many, many years, did not want to see the labor folks had done for that bed cap go to shambles after a pandemic. So one, the fight was to hold the city and the sheriff accountable to the agreements that had already been made: that New Orleans didn't need a jail complex that large; that the building of an additional facility would be going against that 1,438-bed cap. That was number one.

Number two was that in 2021 we were in the middle of a sheriff election. We were going to have a potentially new sheriff starting in 2022. We had Sheriff Marlin Gusman, who was running for reelection and was pro–Phase III because it was in his original plans for the mega-jail he wanted to create. But then you have Susan Hutson running, who was against Phase III.

So in the political realm, we have people who are running for public office on opposing sides of the expansion issue. So people in the community are asking advocates, council, our federal court system, and our judges, whose side do we choose? Because the messaging was so skewed, some folks believed in the plan for a psychiatric facility that was going to be able to help people. And then to have this other candidate, Susan Hutson, a Black woman who is backed by so many criminal-justice community advocates, and she's saying "no Phase III" and going against Gusman, a seventeen-year incumbent. It created a divide in our city, and people didn't really understand what to do. That was the second.

There was also a natural fight that had been happening between the New Orleans City Council, the federal courts, and the sheriff's office. The city council that we had in 2021, the majority opposed the construction of Phase III. But the federal judges, who were in charge of the consent decree for the OJC, were ordering Phase III to be built to come into compliance with the consent decree. We also saw this power struggle between government entities as to who had the authority to say that Phase III had to be built or not. The jail is in District B and the District B council person at the time, Jay Banks, was very against building the jail. The main federal judge, Lance Africk, who was overseeing the decree, was ordering the city to build it. The city council was saying, "You can't force us to build anything in our city if we don't approve it." Then the federal judge was saying, "We're the court—if we say 'build the jail,' you're going to build it." And the federal courts started threatening the council that they would be held in contempt of court.

So we have this multilayered fight. We have this political environment where folks were confused and didn't understand where their voting power lay within this issue and how they should maneuver. We had the community activists saying we had been fighting for a smaller, safer, more humane

OJC for over a decade post-Katrina, and we're not going to just let you throw away all that work. Then there was this governmental power struggle between the council and the courts that was happening.

Also shaping this fight was the deadline for the FEMA funding. FEMA was saying, "Hurricane Katrina hit y'all how many years ago? And y'all are proposing to use sixty-plus million dollars of FEMA funding to build this jail? You need to have a 'considerable amount' of construction done on this building or we're pulling that funding from you." Which means then the city would be responsible for allocating regular budget dollars to build this jail. So there was also this budget process.

All of this was happening simultaneously in 2021. The need to engage with the fight against Phase III was heightened, and there was an opportunity, almost. I really don't like to call it that, but in organizing work sometimes those types of situations create an opportunity for organizers to ramp up, having all these things mix together and create this hyper-awareness of Phase III. Which a lot of people didn't even know was on the table before.

For OPPRC there was a pressure to really be in all these different spaces at one time, trying to advocate in the different respective avenues as to why Phase III was not the way to go. I had to engage in processes that I had never thought I would have to as a social, racial, economic justice organizer. But then I had to be at zoning meetings with the city planning commission. And I had to talk about FEMA funding and the allocation of reconstruction dollars versus a fund balance and budget allocations. I wasn't prepared for that, but we had to do it. We were thrust into this multilayered organizing, and we filled that need well, the best that we could.

Lydia: Can you say a little bit about why most of the city council had come out against Phase III? Also does the mayor fit anywhere in this dynamic?

Lexi: The majority of the city council was against Phase III because we were pushing them to be against Phase III. We're in this space where we are constituents who elect them. We're in their faces. Every city council meeting, every time that this came up in the criminal justice committee meetings, we were there. We were having breakfast with the District B council member at eight-thirty in the morning. Eating shrimp and grits and talking to him about why he cannot allow that jail to be built in his district. It was heavy. New Orleans is such a nuanced organizing space. It is so much about your ability to build relationships and rapport and then match that relationship and rapport with the issue. It is a social city, and those dynamics are important. I think the council felt the pressure from us showing up to meetings, pushing them to have breakfasts and coffee, building the type of relationships where they understood that we had the backing of so many community members. They realized that they would get themselves into a really nasty space come reelection time if they didn't side with the community. Then the other council members, who really were not trying to take a position, had to side with those who were opposed, even without saying so, because they realized the power dynamic happening.

The mayor's office didn't have much power in this. Although the administration was generally favorable toward the Phase III plan in the fall of 2019. But in the summer of 2020, as COVID reduced city revenues, she became more aligned with the council given the long-term costs of Phase III.

What was really happening was that the folks in the city government were scared of the federal judges who were saying they were going to hold them in contempt of court and make them pay fines. I can't remember the exact number, but I think the fines for each city council person were upward of forty-five thousand dollars and potential jail time. As the threats started to be made, I think it felt safer for some folks in office to just not say anything at all than to take a stance one way or another. One way that council maneuvered around it was often to just defer votes past deadlines. It would fall off the docket rather than that they would vote against it. But they didn't vote for it, and that was because of our pressure on them; pushing them to decide without deciding, so that way they could protect themselves from being held in contempt of court, but also so that way they could stay aligned with the community.

Lydia: Was that also partially about running out the clock for those FEMA funds?

Lexi: Yeah, so the federal court ordered that the city file for an extension on the FEMA funds. FEMA came here and wanted to hear from the constituents about why we were so against these funds being used to build a jail. I remember it was six p.m., we're in council chambers, and these FEMA representatives are there asking what is happening. We told them: "Listen, this is not the way we want our communities to receive care, if that's what you're calling this. This is not care. If the sheriff builds this jail, he will fill it. This is not where our most vulnerable community members should have to go." We were advocating for the FEMA funding to be used to build a psychiatric day support facility. We estimated it would cost much less; I believe we estimated ten million dollars to build, and then we said to meet the consent decree, the existing Phase II building could be retrofitted for seven million dollars. And the remainder of the sixty-plus million dollars could be used for community reconstruction and recovery. But the federal judges' pressure was just too much, and FEMA ended up extending the deadline to use the money, I believe, until 2026. And FEMA said that by then a "considerable amount" of construction needed to be done. There needed to be a construction-cost contract, blueprints, a responsible-bidding ordinance, bids from contractors, and a "considerable amount" of construction needed to be completed to keep the FEMA funding. Otherwise, FEMA will pull the funds, and the city will be responsible for paying for the jail construction.

Lydia: Can you tell me about OPPRC's strategizing around this?

Lexi: The first layer of that was really education. Folks in the community needed to know what was happening. There was this status quo thing with Marlin Gusman having been sheriff for seventeen years, where he could really do what he wanted and go untouched. As a 501(c)(3) organization, we couldn't endorse a candidate. So the first piece of strategy was educating our community on what a potential shift in leadership could look like, regardless of who was in that leadership position. OPPRC created a table, a larger coalition, of organizations across the city, some focused on criminal justice work, but a lot of intersecting organizations, economic justice, mental health activists, housing activists, etc. It was over fifty organizations that came together and through a monthly conversation built a sheriff platform. This platform basically outlined what we wanted to see in a sheriff, and a heavy piece of that was somebody who would be against building Phase III. We then pushed that platform out with our communications and education campaign.

In addition, there was a simultaneous campaign that OPPRC was running called Help Not Handcuffs that was advocating for a non-police crisis-response team for mental health crises in the city. There was this marriage, almost, of access for those in our city who were dealing with mental health crises to receive completely non-carceral care. From that advocacy—which included forums and education meetings in every district, both virtually and in person for months, with hundreds attending, where we helped to educate the community about what it looks like to receive dignified and non-carceral mental health support and care from beginning to end—we were able to reach such a wide group of folks who we brought into the conversation around the sheriff's campaign. Then for the campaign we also held forums where we invited all the candidates who were running for sheriff. And, of course, Gusman never came. He would never respond to our emails. Then what would end up happening is the candidates who did show up would then be asked questions based off our community-centered and -endorsed platform. They would have to tell the community if they aligned with the platform that they built, including opposing the construction of Phase III.

So the constituents that were going to be voting were really voting issue-based instead of candidate-based. Which was a very important organizing tool. We never said who to vote for. But we did tell you collectively what the community wanted from the person in that role. It was up to the people who were running for office to decide if they were going to give the people that or not. So that was a large tactic at the beginning. The other side of it was the city government organizing: so many conversations, us at OPPRC writing and drafting ordinances for city council members to introduce and endorse so that we could prolong the process. It was having tons of meetings with advocates who had maneuvered these situations in other municipalities, and really building a strategy that kept those in city government safe from the federal court threats while allowing us to run the clock out on the need to vote either for or against building Phase III.

Then the next layer was the city planning commission layer —getting the city planning commission to go against approving the land to build Phase III. If the city government and the federal courts couldn't get that space zoned to build that type of building, they weren't going to be able to build it. If you can't get the zoning permit, you can't put bids out. You can't put bids out, you can't build. That was a large strategy, and honestly a new one to me. I had never engaged in that type of strategizing before as far as dealing with zoning ordinances and documents. We put so much pressure on the city planning commission that many people abstained from voting, and they ended up not voting either way. In an unprecedented vote, the planning commission decided to give no recommendation at all, which rarely happens. What that created then was the situation for the city council to say because we don't have a recommendation from the city planning commission on whether or not to zone, we are going to keep deferring and keep deferring until it's deferred past the deadline. Then what would have to happen was the city council would need to reintroduce an ordinance, and they could again defer and defer past the deadline, and then you'd have to reintroduce everything all over again. It created this ability to hold everybody in their own respective sectors, if you will, accountable to what the community was advocating for. It allowed them to follow a due process in city government, where they basically had to start over and over again and they never got anywhere. That was really the strategy. It was just to hold people where they were at and if we could maintain that, we could successfully halt the construction of that jail, which we did for years.

Lydia: What happened next? Where are things at now?

Lexi: In a wild turn of events, New Orleans ousted Marlin Gusman and elected Susan Hutson, who was self-proclaimed as a progressive and anti–Phase III. This was a huge win for organizers across the city. Decades and decades of labor made this possible. It was amazing to see.

And then came the city council election. It was on the same ballot. Almost everyone on city council that was opposed to Phase III was voted off. We started 2022 with a new sheriff and a new council. I sat on Susan Hutson's transition committee, and the transition was awful. Gusman did not allow an appropriate succession. The new sheriff wasn't allowed access to the jail. She wasn't allowed to go in the jail. The transition committee wasn't allowed to go in the jail. For months. We weren't given documents. We weren't given records. We were really gridlocked. There was nothing that we could do to start to try to continue the fight against Phase III from the inside, which would have been the ideal strategy, because we were just locked out of being able to have access.

Then there was an entirely new council, most of whom are lawyers, which was an interesting dynamic change. So you had almost every single council person saying, "We're not going against the federal court. It doesn't matter if we're opposed to Phase III or not, individually. We're lawyers, and we know what being held in contempt of court looks like, and we're not doing it. This is a legal issue, and we're not going against the federal judges." Whereas the prior council were like, "We'll challenge it because the community is telling us to challenge it." These new council members didn't feel that same pressure, and they were very aware and afraid of the legal ramifications of pushing against the federal courts. They weren't willing to engage in that push. I think it was too much of a polarizing issue for that new council. And the folks in power on the council, the council president, the vice president, the District B member, were all saying if the majority of us don't feel comfortable [pushing the courts], we're not going to do it. This council is also a little bit more pro-carceral. We have a couple of members now who are very pro-NOPD [New Orleans Police Department] and at every council meeting are using their platform to say, "Join the police force, join OPSO, become a deputy. This is how we stop crime."

Lydia: Because there's also all the crime/moral-panic stuff running rampant …

Lexi: Right, and that would be a whole different long conversation about the pushback narrative that was happening around public safety and "crime." While we were providing education about what was actually happening in the city, our new council was coming in and saying, "There's a crime surge and New Orleans isn't safe, and our police department is under a consent decree so they can't actually do their job. We need to support them instead of defunding them." The messaging was "Everybody in New Orleans, now that this election is over, be terrified of what happens if we don't have police, if we don't have jail."

Then what we have seen now with the new sheriff's finally transitioning into the role. In her first ninety days, she's realizing nothing is what we thought it was inside of the jail. It's in shambles. It's understaffed. It's got poor sanitation. No laundry. No library. So the people that are currently incarcerated there are suffering. So then her focus shifts from advocating against Phase III to taking care of what she currently is dealing with inside.

And after the election, I'm of the opinion that the organizers and advocates that had just worked this past year and a half in the middle of a pandemic—or I will speak for myself—personally, I needed to take a breath. I had been working seventeen-hour days. And that need to take a breath created a gap of pressure, and with the crime-surge narrative being spun with entirely new council people, a lot of advocates did not have relationships, the transition of the sheriff being as horrific as it was, and the jail being in a sort of emergency situation, the priority to fight against Phase III decreased greatly. As of now [in spring 2023], there has not been any public acknowledgment of where the sheriff's office or the federal court is with the construction of Phase III. I have not seen any additional zoning information, nor have I seen it come up in council meetings. I think folks are kind of letting this cool down a little bit and doing things out of the public eye, so as not to start a movement around this again.

This is an important thing to remember for organizing: Part of strategy and movement-building, especially in abolition work, is ensuring that you have a wide enough network of individuals working toward the same common goal that you can deploy in intervals. Because if there's a lesson that I've learned over the past year or two years of fighting Phase III in New Orleans, it is that when we come together, we know how to come together. But we often are in such a moment of crisis that we are not thinking about how to remain sustainable. What happened was all these organizations citywide were so full-force for so many months of this campaign that everyone needed a moment. But when everyone took a moment at the same time, the momentum was lost. The pressure was lost. There was no way that any of us could have been well and continued to function at the level that we were functioning. If I can give any reflections for advice, it's to be sure that as you're strategizing in your campaigns, in your teams, in your coalitions, that you are always thinking about and centering sustainability. How are we going to ensure that this lives past us? How are we going to ensure that there's enough decentralization of information and knowledge that if I were to need to step away and take care of myself, that someone could pick right up where I left off? And that I know who those people are. They're identified. There's commitment there. There's a continuum of that pressure and that labor there. Because we often see this in our movement spaces. There's a really large push. This happened when George Floyd was murdered. There are hundreds and thousands of people showing up, all unified around the same effort. And then there's a need for those folks to take a second, because they're exhausted. And when they take that second, we lose a little bit of momentum. It is a strategy of the folks in power and it's a good one. To wear out people. We take that little moment, two days to sleep, take off one city council meeting, and in that one city council meeting they're passing five ordinances that knock us back six steps. But if I were to ensure that there were five people there who weren't exhausted when I needed to take off that one or two council meetings, that might not happen.

So no Phase III has been built yet, but I don't know what the future is. I personally will continue to be engaged. I want to be a part of creating a continuum of knowledge and access to that information. I hope that as we continue as a city to fight for more humane and just ways of taking care of our folks, that people really center what just happened over the past couple of years. Even if this building ends up being built, it would have been built eleven years ago if we hadn't fought against it. That is in itself a success for a myriad of reasons in the South, in one of the most incarcerated cities in one of the most incarcerated states in the United States.

10

Real Solutions: Organizing for Alternatives to a Big New Jail in a Small Republican County

Sarah Westover and Matt Witt

In May 2020, a community coalition in a rural and small-town Republican county in southern Oregon soundly defeated a ballot measure to fund a new jail that would have had three times the capacity of the existing facility. The measure was placed on the ballot by the three county commissioners—all Republicans—and the campaign to pass it was spearheaded by the popular county sheriff, also a Republican. It was endorsed by the city councils in ten of the eleven incorporated towns in the county and backed by the local newspaper on both its editorial and news pages. Yet voters turned it down by a nearly three-to-one margin.

Every campaign has its own particular set of circumstances, but the following are some of the key ingredients that produced this particular victory.

1. **Build a broad coalition based on common goals,** even if coalition partners don't agree on every criminal justice issue.

2. **Offer an alternative** of real solutions instead of "just say no," and cite the experience of other local jurisdictions to show that those solutions are not just theories but have been proven in practice.

3. **Provide factual data** and point out that the county failed to do so, while avoiding personal attacks.

4. **Set aside partisan politics** and be willing to work with interested Republicans and to challenge Democratic officials who are pro-jail or unwilling to take a stand at all.

5. **Anticipate and inoculate against the arguments of jail proponents** so they don't get to frame the debate.

6. **Find ways to communicate through traditional media** even if they are biased in favor of jail capacity expansion.

7. **Use social media to provide information** and not to get into conflicts with people who will never be convinced.

8. **Help local residents who are not the "usual suspects" to gain the information and confidence to speak out** at hearings and public meetings, through emails and phone calls, and in the media.

9. **Use the campaign to build support to adopt real solutions after the vote** (and not just to defeat a backward step) and continue to bring in new people afterward to strengthen the coalition.

10. **Elect supporters of real solutions to local offices.**

We expand on each of these approaches later after providing background information on Jackson County, where this battle took place, and on the proposal for a big new jail.

A Republican County with Low Wages, High Housing Costs, Addiction, and Mental Illness

Jackson County, located on Oregon's southern border about 300 miles from Portland, has a population of about 225,000 people. It has one town of about 85,000 (Medford), two of about 20,000 (Ashland and Central Point), and eight smaller incorporated towns. Nearly one-third of its residents live in unincorporated rural areas. Republicans win every election for the three county commissioner positions, no matter who the candidates are. Election of a Tea Party hardliner in 2014 has pushed the other Republicans further to the right.

Like the rest of the West, the county was originally inhabited by Indigenous tribes (in this case, the Shasta, Takelma, and Latgawa), but white settlers arrived in droves in the 1850s after gold was discovered. The region eventually became a center for logging and agriculture, with an increased dependence in recent decades on Latinx immigrant workers. At least up to now, the climate has been ideal for vineyards as well as for cannabis and hemp cultivation that have surged as a result of legalization.

In recent years, developers have profited by building housing for retirees from California and elsewhere. At the same time, the wood products industry's failure to manage forests sustainably contributed to a shift from relatively high-wage timber jobs to low-wage, nonunion jobs in tourism and service industries. Today, median income in Jackson County is 24 percent lower than the national average. Yet the median home price is 9 percent higher than the national average, and one out of three households pays more than half its income for housing.

Like other non-urban areas, the county has a problem with meth addiction, production, and distribution. A study released in January 2022 by the Substance Abuse and Mental Health Services Administration found that Oregon ranks second in the country for most substance use disorders but fiftieth in access to treatment. Similarly, Oregon was the worst state in Mental Health America's ranking that combines prevalence of mental illness and lack of access to services.

The County's Campaign for a New, Triple-Size Jail

The existing Jackson County jail, built in 1981, originally had room for 176 men and women. The county has since expanded capacity to the current 300. The jail holds people who are awaiting trial, serving short sentences, or are in violation of probation or parole requirements.

It has long been a county goal to create separate taxing districts for the library system and for the jail so each would have its own permanent revenue stream. This would allow the county administrator and county commissioners to continue to portray themselves as fiscally responsible guardians of the general fund, which they could use for other purposes. They succeeded in 2014 in creating such a separate tax for the libraries.

In 2018, a new sheriff in his early forties was elected by a three-to-one margin. He had broad support across the political spectrum and presented himself as an evidence-based moderate, in contrast to a controversial sheriff who had served for twelve years during which the county spent at least $93,000 litigating and settling cases against the jail, according to an investigative report by local television station KOBI. With the new sheriff in place, the Republican county commissioners and county administrator decided that the political climate was right to try to pass a ballot measure to raise county property taxes by more than 40 percent to fund a new, separate taxing district to build and operate a new jail with three times more capacity.

County officials paid for a professional public opinion poll to test the arguments they were considering. (No arguments in opposition were tested.) The principal finding of the poll was that the county could not simply rely on its Republican registration majority in order to win. While some of its base would be in favor due to concerns about crime, others would lean toward voting no because of concerns about taxes. The county would need to win substantial support among "key demographic groups that often support tax increases," such as Democrats, women, and voters under thirty.

Armed with that strategic advice, the county set about trying to build a majority electoral coalition for its jail tax district proposal that would include those less conservative groups. The county strategists used the following tactics:

They made the new sheriff their principal spokesperson, rather than the county commissioners who would be seen as more partisan by Democratic voters.

They designed their message to appeal to liberals—that a newer jail would be more humane, and that a bigger jail would allow the county to hold people long enough to connect them to services for mental illness and addiction (although the new taxing district would be set up in a way that none of the new tax could be used to expand or improve those services).

They pressured city councils in the eleven incorporated towns in the county, including the few towns that have Democratic voter registration majorities, to pass a resolution that endorsed the measure. That pressure campaign included a threat that the county would cut off certain kinds of cooperation with the police force of any city whose council did not get on board.

They systematically wooed key council members in the two more liberal cities in private meetings. This occurred at a time when some of those council members were potentially in line to run for mayor in their towns with the support of the business community. Those council members, who had personal ties and credibility in their towns, became key spokespersons for a "yes" vote.

They set up an "advisory committee" of local agencies and elected leaders that was portrayed in the media as an attempt to get broad input. In practice, the "committee" met only a few times and its "meetings" consisted of presentations about why a new and bigger jail was needed.

They arranged active support from the local newspaper. This included editorials and a three-part front-page series about individuals who were grateful that they had been jailed because it provided the kick in the pants they needed to turn their life around.

They issued a news release two weeks before the vote saying the jail had had to release two undocumented Mexicans charged with transporting twenty pounds of meth because "we have too many offenders and not enough bed space."

This campaign by the county might have succeeded had it not been for a countercampaign by the anti-jail-expansion coalition described below.

The "Real Solutions" Campaign for Alternatives to More Jail Capacity

The challenge for opponents of the new, bigger jail was the mirror image of the challenge facing the county. Opponents needed to both hold a large majority of Democratic voters and at the same time appeal to a significant number of Republicans. Here, we detail ten key ingredients to the campaign.

1. **Build a broad coalition based on common goals, even if coalition partners don't agree on every criminal justice issue.** A "Real Solutions" coalition came together to develop and implement strategy and divide up the work. It included mental health advocates from the local chapter of the National Alliance on Mental Illness (NAMI) who were primarily oriented toward working within the system to get small concessions, organizers from a community organizing hub called the Rogue Action Center with experience building public pressure for systems change, and some of the few progressive elected officials in local communities. Each had expertise to contribute to the campaign. Some might have settled for a promise of an additional social worker or two based in a new jail. Others in the community wanted to push for shifting funds away from law enforcement to fund alternative programs. Frequent communication was crucial to maintain unity and trust around a focused goal of defeating the new, bigger jail and laying the groundwork for crisis intervention programs and other reforms.

2. **Offer an alternative of real solutions instead of "just say no," and cite the experience of other local jurisdictions** to show that those solutions are not just theories but have been proven in practice. If the county had been able to make the vote only about the current jail vs. a new, supposedly more modern jail, it might have won. Some significant percentage of Democrats might have been persuaded that "more humane" is better than less humane, and some significant number of Republicans might have been convinced that if you don't want more crime as the county's population grows, there is no alternative but a bigger jail.

For all of these voter groups, it was crucial to show that there was a more practical and cost-effective alternative while also demonstrating that the county's plan would actually do more harm than good. The Real Solutions coalition argued that:

- A new, bigger jail would soon be overcrowded because underlying causes were not being addressed, including mental illness, addiction, homelessness, and poverty.
- Evidence shows that being jailed, and being held for longer periods, makes recidivism more likely, not less—in part because it creates new trauma and new barriers to getting jobs, rental housing, and needed benefits.
- Other counties have adopted more effective approaches to reduce the number of people jailed in the first place, reduce repeat offenses, save money, and provide better prevention, diversion, crisis assistance, and treatment.
- A huge new expenditure for a triple-size jail would make it far less likely that the county would ever fund more effective alternatives that have been implemented elsewhere.

To shine a spotlight on proven alternatives, the Rogue Action Center and the local NAMI chapter organized several public presentations featuring law enforcement leaders from other counties who explained that they have been able to reduce jail bookings instead of expanding jails. In many situations, they said, a response by mental health professionals or social service workers is more effective and less costly than a response by police.

Tad Larson, the jail commander from Marion County, Oregon, explained at one of those forums that his county operates a mobile crisis team that partners mental health professionals with law enforcement. The Crisis Outreach Response Team, a collaboration of the Marion County Sheriff's Office and the Health Department, connects individuals with counseling services, alcohol and drug treatment, and peer mentor support as an alternative to jail time. Less than 3 percent of calls the crisis teams respond to result in arrests, Larson reported, and Marion County has reduced annual jail bookings by 20 to 25 percent.

At another Real Solutions forum, Jackson County residents learned about a crisis intervention program in Lane County called Cahoots (Crisis Assistance Helping Out on the Streets) that responds to 24,000 calls per year and provides 24/7 free response for non-emergency medical care or first aid, dispute resolution and conflict mediation, and a broad range of non-criminal crises, including homelessness, intoxication, disorientation, substance abuse, and mental illness problems. According to program coordinator Tim Black, the program saves $15.5 million a year by handling calls that would otherwise go to the police, reducing arrests, and diverting patients from emergency rooms.

The county had a hard time trying to discredit these examples of alternative solutions that work, arguing at various times that 1) the county had no money for alternative programs (even as it was proposing a major tax increase for a new jail); 2) that problems like homelessness, mental illness, and addiction were already being addressed in the county (a claim which defied any voter's common sense); 3) that it was the responsibility of other agencies, and not the county, to address those problems (which just came across as finger pointing instead of problem solving); or 4) that while other counties might be making progress on those issues, Jackson County is so unique in undefined ways that solutions being used elsewhere wouldn't work.

3. Provide factual data and point out that the county failed to do so, while avoiding personal attacks. The Real Solutions coalition pointed out that the county had not provided voters with studies showing the projected impact of a new, bigger jail, nor had it done studies of alternative approaches.

By contrast, the coalition publicized studies like "Broken Ground" by the Vera Institute of Justice, which analyzed the experience of seventy-seven counties and found that "larger jails often become overcrowded again because expansion fails to address the root causes of increased [jail] population."

The coalition also pointed to a Marion County study showing that the two-year rate for low-risk defendants reoffending hovers at around 17 percent when they are kept in jail for two to three days, but spikes to 51 percent once jail stays increase to two weeks.

In the small towns and rural areas where this debate took place, fact-based arguments went over better than personal criticisms of the sheriff or other county officials would have and kept those officials from playing the victim to distract voters from the real issues.

4. Set aside partisan politics and be willing to work with interested Republicans and to challenge Democratic officials who are pro-jail or unwilling to take a stand at all. The coalition repeatedly pointed out that crisis intervention alternatives are supported by a national group called Right on Crime founded by well-known Republicans such as Newt Gingrich, Grover Norquist, Asa Hutchinson, and Mike Huckabee—political figures with whom most coalition activists have little in common on other issues.

At the same time, community members were willing in both public meetings and private communication to challenge Democratic leaders who did not want to offend local law enforcement or county officials.

5. Anticipate and inoculate against pro-jail arguments so proponents don't get to frame the debate. As an example, it was obvious that the county planned to rely heavily on a simple mathematical argument that the county population had grown by two-thirds since the current jail was built and therefore a bigger one was clearly needed. The coalition got ahead of that by pointing out that the county's population will continue to grow going forward, making alternatives to incarceration even more essential unless voters want to constantly pay for bigger and bigger jails.

6. Find ways to communicate through traditional media even if they are biased in favor of jail expansion. Instead of writing off the local newspaper because it was using both its news pages and editorial page to support the jail tax, those who wanted alternatives to a new, bigger jail did the best they could to get their message into the paper. Over the course of a year and a half, eight guest opinion pieces by different authors opposing the jail tax were submitted and published. Only one was submitted by someone in favor of the jail tax, and that author did not even live in the county. Many other residents successfully submitted letters to the editor. In addition, the paper felt compelled to cover the community forums the coalition organized that featured law enforcement officials from other counties.

7. Use social media to provide information and not to get into conflicts with people who will never be convinced. Real Solutions supporters made key points and sources easily available online to help others talk to their family members, friends, coworkers, and neighbors, and spent no time on pointless "debates" with trolls who would never change their mind anyway.

8. **Help local residents who are not the "usual suspects" to gain the information and confidence to speak out** at hearings and public meetings, through emails and phone calls, and in the media. This takes personal contact and phone calls, not just posting notices and hoping other residents will take action. While the coalition had intended to canvas door to door before the vote, targeting low-income neighborhoods that are hardest hit both by crime and by over-incarceration for conversations about better alternatives to the jail tax, the COVID pandemic took away that vital tool.

Opponents of the jail tax who spoke at county hearings outnumbered residents speaking in favor by a ratio of fifty to four. At a county commissioners' meeting toward the end of the campaign where the Tea Party commissioner broke ranks and spoke against the jail tax measure, she cited the overwhelming number of opposition calls and emails she had received. She said, "I can count on the fingers of one hand the people who support it."

9. **Use the campaign to build support to adopt real solutions after the vote and continue to bring in new people.** A great deal of time and effort went into the Real Solutions campaign before the vote on the proposed jail tax. It was important to make sure that the result was to build momentum for a better alternative, which was the coalition's ultimate goal, and not just to stop a backward step.

The Real Solutions Coalition has continued to organize since the vote. It has held several more community forums to continue to educate residents about crisis intervention services and other solutions that are needed. It also has recruited dozens of additional supporters who have helped keep up pressure on local officials to implement alternatives.

10. **Elect supporters of real solutions to local offices.** A key to victory was that progressives had made an effort in the preceding years to recruit and support candidates for city council and mayor in some of the county's towns. On three of those city councils they were in the minority but still were able to make information requests and provide important perspectives during public meetings. In the small town of Talent, the mayor and three city councilors formed a majority that had the courage to refuse to endorse the jail plan, despite pressure from law enforcement. That vote served as a beacon to other county residents and undermined the county's strategy of roping in all the towns first.

Organizing in the Aftermath of the New Jail's Defeat

The ballot measure lost by 71 percent to 29 percent, but we all know that there are rarely permanent victories or permanent defeats. The Jackson County sheriff and county administrator still want a big new jail, funded by its own tax increase to create a permanent, independent revenue stream.

Their first step after the defeat was to attempt reprisals against the few local elected officials who had opposed the ballot measure. They saw their first opportunity just days after the vote when George Floyd was murdered by police in Minneapolis and a member of the Talent city council who had voted against the new jail posted an angry reaction to the Floyd murder on her personal Facebook page that was then "liked" by the mayor. At the next city council meeting, the law enforcement community called on both officials to resign and implied that Talent might be left without police coverage if they did not. The local newspaper chimed in as well.

This particular attack on jail tax opponents ultimately fell flat, given that Talent residents were overwhelmingly opposed to the ballot measure. In fact, within months the three council members who had supported a triple-size new jail had all either resigned or decided not to run for reelection and had been replaced by more progressive residents.

Law enforcement officials were more successful in more conservative Medford. The council member who had been most outspoken against the ballot measure was defeated by a Black deputy sheriff who ran against her in a four-way race. They also succeeded in getting a former police chief elected as Medford's new mayor.

They also saw an opportunity to lay the groundwork for another try at a big new jail when illegal cannabis and hemp grows surged in the county just as climate-fueled drought, fires, and smoke were getting more severe. Republican and Democratic officials began a coordinated public relations campaign against heavily armed "cartels" that had "invaded" the region and were stealing water, undermining legal growers, and committing human rights violations against their workers. The state Democratic leadership responded with funds for more sheriff's deputies. It wasn't hard to see how this racialized campaign could eventually lead to bipartisan calls for more jail capacity.

At the same time, the Real Solutions campaign appeared to be moving officials at the county and the city of Medford to consider the kinds of alternatives the coalition had highlighted. They shifted from "we already do that" or "that won't work here" to actual planning meetings about possible crisis intervention and community court programs like other counties have.

The coalition pushed to overcome official resistance to community participation in that planning, and put forward a clear set of criteria for such programs in order to make it harder for new solutions to be so watered down that they would not work.

By the end of 2022, the county had launched a mobile crisis team program overseen by mental health providers, hospital representatives, county officials, community members active in the Real Solutions Coalition, and others. That group had a

Community Engagement Committee that was reaching out to underserved communities to identify needs.

Organizing for real solutions and not a big new jail in Jackson County also contributed to the decision by the Oregon legislature in 2021 to appropriate $10 million to expand local mobile crisis programs throughout the state. The Real Solutions coalition's success also helped push Oregon's members of Congress to get the federal government to award grants totaling $15 million to twenty states to help local jurisdictions plan crisis response alternatives.

At some point, local officials in Jackson County may adopt some of the coalition's proposals and then incorporate that progress into messaging designed once again to build a voter majority for a triple-size new jail—"we did what you wanted but we still need a new jail." But as of the end of 2022, that remains a battle for the future.

11

Lessons from the No New Jails Network and the New York City Struggle Against Carceral Feminism

An Interview with Mon Mohapatra of the No New Jails Network

Judah Schept: To start us off, can you tell us about the No New Jails Network (NNJN) and its origins, mission, and the motivation for it?

Mon Mohapatra: The No New Jails Network (NNJN), which was originally called No New Jails National Network, started officially in 2020. It was inspired a lot by the George Floyd/Breonna Taylor uprisings, and this sense of needing to connect across locations and cities and different campaigns. We were just coming out of the No New Jails NYC campaign, where one of the oversights had been to not connect with people who had been organizing against jail expansion in other cities and learn from them. The uprising made all of these struggles seem like they were shared, including amongst folks organizing against jail expansion or to close down a jail in places like Los Angeles, or St. Louis, or New Orleans, or Bangor. NNJN came together with an original group of about ten people, including people who had been organizing in Kentucky; Maine; New York; Orange County; in Georgia with Stop the Jail ATL; in Washington, DC, with No New Jails DC; and people from Fight Toxic Prisons.

We wanted to be intentional about making sure that it wasn't just bicoastal. The goal was to create a network, similar to the National Bail Fund Network, where we would be able to share strategies, discuss emerging issues, and take an explicitly abolitionist approach to stopping the construction of new jails and [pursuing] the closing down of old ones. That element of it, that it should be explicitly abolitionist, was one of the most important aspects, because a lot of the organizers were coming to this disillusioned by the reformist energy within their own campaigns or in their own localities. The idea was that we would all get together and have conversations about some of these dynamics related to abolition and reform, ways to respond to these dynamics, and potentially scale up a little bit together.

In that initial year, which was 2021, we spent most of our time setting up the structure for the network. We set it up to have a larger audience through the listserv, and a more operational team that would have two people from each of the campaigns. We wanted it to be a rotating central infrastructure so that people from different campaigns had a chance to join and participate in the management of the network, and also to ensure that someone didn't just join once and then disappear from the network. So we spent a lot of time setting up the governance and management structure, how we wanted to communicate with each other, and determining our first year's organizing priorities. Those priorities included ideas like producing a map of different jail expansion campaigns, beginning an archive, producing a website that had a manifesto, and holding strategy sessions to think about the dynamics and patterns in all of these campaigns. I think it changed a little bit in its second year, which was 2022. We focused on doing political education together, events, and learning. There was still some strategizing together, but a lot of "Okay, so we've identified that things like carceral humanism are coming up in a lot of campaigns, what can we do to learn about this?" I think there were a lot of lessons to be learned about the nature of organizing around jail construction and expansion itself that impacted the network's design and mission. If the network continues to exist, we'll probably need to change its goals and vision to be able to meet the organizing moment.

Lydia Pelot-Hobbs: Could you say more about the continuities and differences across different geographies that folks fighting jails are experiencing? Both in terms of states like New York or California versus a place like Kentucky, but also bigger cities versus more suburban or rural areas?

Mon: I think one of the strategy questions that is shared across the board concerns the most effective organizing structure for fighting for decarceration. So one example of that is the concept of coalitions versus campaigns versus something else; i.e., the organizing structure within which you are actually trying to fight against something. People have not figured out the right way to do this. Which isn't to say that there's a lot of wrong ways. I think questions that come up for folks include: "Do we need to build a nonprofit? Should we be a mutual aid organization that's specifically focusing on mutual aid with prisoners, and then from that to build a campaign? Is a campaign even effective when some of these things are like ten or twenty years in the making? Is a coalition what we need to be doing when some people are abolitionists and others are completely not, when some people really want to do electoral work, and others don't?" Where people land on these questions is different across the different geographies. But this is a big question for organizing that I think requires more resources to figure out.

In addition, it is really hard to have the conversation about jail population and numbers of jail beds or stuff like that at the same register across different geographies, when you're also dealing with the fact that one group is a nonprofit, and one group is like three people in a mutual aid organization.

Even something like Critical Resistance, a relatively more established, formal organization that has a lot of these grassroots relationships, is still different from a group of five people in Oklahoma who are learning about abolitionist politics as they go. They're incredible organizers, because they're catching up quickly. But it's not the same conversation that's being had. And there's just a difference in understanding some of the strategies. Some people are just trying out certain strategies like divest/invest for the first time, and other people are like, we stopped doing divest/invest six years ago, because we realized it was problematic. That kind of thing makes it challenging to find shared strategies. I don't think it's impossible, but it definitely makes it hard.

One important commonality across geographies are the trends in carceral humanism, carceral ableism, and sanism, the concept of psychiatric benefits from jailing and mental health treatment through incarceration. It was happening in Orange County, Santa Clara, Sacramento, DC, New Orleans, New York, Austin. A lot of organizing had to focus on organizing doctors and other medical professionals to push back on the idea that a jail can be a mental health facility. The reasons for that are different because there are different demographics. In some places, right-wing politics are more common. In other places, the level of homelessness and mental health needs are just high. So the reason why they're using this narrative is different. But the deployment of that narrative to justify jail construction or renovation or more funding to the department of corrections is pretty common.

Another commonality is conditions litigation. Almost every group that was involved with the network has had a history of using litigation to address either overcrowding or use of force, which has either backfired or been inconsistent with abolitionist strategy in the long run. Rikers is a good example where the consent decree on use of force in Rikers was supposed to stop the use and abuse of force inside Rikers after the death of Kalief Browder. But then the city manipulated that into an expansionist argument: "Oh, overcrowding is a problem. Violence is a problem. Corrections officers aren't being taken care of. We need to build new jails with better staff, more space, more health care allocations." And that's a dynamic shared around [the country]. The conditions are bad. There's overcrowding. There's no healthcare. The staff are abusive. And so organizers sue, but then the city or county uses the lawsuit to push for a new jail or for renovations, or to invite investments in their correctional capacity. And that goes hand in hand with arguments around overcrowding conditions, like cities getting renovations and new jails, for being compliant with ADA [Americans with Disabilities Act] policies, which is also pretty common. Another common theme involves the pursuit of "more beautiful" jails, like a carceral campus. So in a lot of places where they are building new county or city jails, it's because they're like, "the old ones are just ugly" or "they don't represent modern jailing and we could modernize our carceral system."

Another similarity across geographies is the internal difficulty within campaigns and coalitions between reformist reforms and non-reformist or abolitionist reforms, between people who think that mutual aid is the strategy and people who think that we need to be doing political lobbying and rallies, between people who think that there needs to be a better survivor politic that's pro survivor and people who are like, "No, we just need to be bailing everybody out." These challenges around the actual strategies, while they're different in different places, speak to internal differences within campaigns, and we don't know how to resolve them. We don't know how to deal with conflict in our campaigns. And we didn't set ourselves up for a ten- or twenty-year project. We set ourselves up for a one-year campaign, and so have encountered a lot of challenges. Some of these difficulties are people just not knowing everybody in this organizing structure or campaign, or not having the same understanding of some of the dynamics, like transphobia, or not having the same understanding of the things that are causing people to go into jail in the first place. And that is an organizing challenge for people.

Judah: I wanted to follow up and ask if the patterns and differences you observed map onto certain identifiable things like scale or geography? And were there some strategies or ways of organizing that you thought were more successful than others?

Mon: One of the differences which I have already named was the kind of organizing structure and the level of wealth or funding that the campaigns have. But I think one of the other big differences is the organizing environment itself. This is a question of geography, to some extent, political geography at least. So for example, somewhere like Los Angeles or New York, the dynamics that people are coming up against are massive foundation-funded organizations, prestigious organizations, as well as organizations that are led by formerly incarcerated people, especially people who have been through the jails themselves. Overall, it's just a heavy nonprofit presence, which is one of the counterinsurgent aspects of these organizing environments. And other places like Madison, Austin, and some of the other towns have campaigns that are ten people with a chapter of a local organization. So this was a challenge for the NNJN: how do we have the same conversations when we're dealing with such different political geographies? The strategies and choices are not going to be the same. This actually came up in the talk that you did, Judah, when someone asked, "Should we appeal to conservatives, and their potential reluctance around jail funding?" And meanwhile, other people were like, "Why would we ever do that?" But the person who asked that question was from a small town that's more than 90 percent white. And so that dynamic, I think it's valuable to explore, but it's definitely been a challenge.

Another big difference is the people who choose to organize around jail expansion or stopping new jail construction do not all share the same politics around it. Someone might come to the conversation and say, "I'm an abolitionist; I think all of this just shouldn't exist." And someone else might come to the conversation from a different city and say, "We don't use the word 'abolition' in our organizing, because it automatically alienates people." And these differences presented a challenge. On a larger scale, this is also related to how we think about solutions. One of the lessons from NNJN has been that there isn't enough experience or resources to help organizers discern what are reformist strategies. When the network came together, many of us expected to identify a pretty clear approach toward principled abolitionist strategies. What happened in practice was that some people identified alternatives to sentencing and to incarceration as really valuable to endorse toward building long-term relationships with allied organizations. And some people were like, "No, we want to fight against all of these things." That has been a real challenge and is also a big difference across campaigns. It's hard to declare yourself an abolitionist network when you can't have people commit to one kind of strategy, because the nature of these campaigns is so different. It hasn't been easy to name those things and challenge them. And there's not really a place, I think, in the movement to do that.

And the last difference was the informality of some of this work that isn't captured in formal organizing structures. So let's say you have No New Jails NYC, which is not existent anymore, but two people show up from that campaign to NNJN. But there's actually three hundred other people in New York City organizing around Rikers. It almost felt like some of the conversations were kind of limited by thinking of this organizing as formal. It's amazing that there are campaigns in all of these places, but it almost felt like sometimes there was an erasure of all the different ways people were actually resisting and participating in the closure or participating in the stopping of an expansion plan that we couldn't really capture in our conversations.

I would say the biggest challenge is not something that's specific to geography and scale, which is that people are willing to make different kinds of compromises in different places. And there is not a kind of shared assessment or gauge for the usefulness of some of these compromises. And that certainly for me is going to be one of the biggest challenges in thinking about some of this stuff. I think it's just a matter of where you are. You're going to be in a campaign that's met with a lot of repression, a lot of backlash, and a lot of co-optation. You're probably going to be campaigning, to some extent, against people who have been through jail. It's hard not to be pushed into making certain kinds of compromises. But maybe because there's a lack of archives, or maybe because people aren't openly talking about this, it's hard to know if some of those compromises are worth it.

Lydia: As a quick follow up to that, is this also an assessment question? Is there space for reflection, for folks to try to assess what worked and what didn't?

Mon: That's a really good question. We have slowly been trying to create an online archive of some of the campaigns and organizing, including some oral storytelling as well as standard details of what a given group did and what worked. I think one of the first challenges with bringing together a group of like-minded organizers from around the country to strategize collectively on responding to jail expansion was to determine the role of an abolitionist politics within that. Many of us are in complicated geographies where it's not always possible to find twenty, thirty committed, studied, abolitionist organizers or groups who have the energy, resources, and time to dedicate to the years, usually decades, that these campaigns end up taking. Others are in places where it's incredibly important to home in on a clear and principled abolitionist analysis in order to counteract carceral and reformist proposals. The goal of the network was to provide a space for organizing that would always demand an end to pretrial detention and that we need to free them all— yet this could be seen by some as an obstacle to materially organizing in their places. We had several conversations as a group about whether to reach out to groups who either don't identify publicly as abolitionist, or who have vital local decarceral campaigns but whose strategies will inevitably expand the scope of the carceral state, as well as conversations about our limited authority as a group. We, of course, didn't know every group or person involved in this work. I think preexisting assessments have been incredibly helpful for work like this, including Detention Watch Network's abolitionist steps to end immigrant detention and CR's nonreformist reforms versus reformist reforms or Up End Movement's Abolitionist Steps to End Family Policing, and creating a method or tool to determine in more detail what it looks like to organize against pretrial detention without expanding social control or supervision would be useful in the long run. Hopefully this book will help with this. In practice, however, there are no clean-cut rules, only complex negotiations and discussions over coalitions, partners, and principles. Particularly in this moment, as many campaigns and anti-jail organizers navigate the counterinsurgent impact of philanthropy and the nonprofit industrial complex, the increasing professionalization of abolitionist organizing, the importance of relational methods and accountability, and internal conflict within the groups anchoring these efforts, there appears to be a need to be both clear in vision and expansive in strategies.

One last thing I'll say as one of my biggest takeaways was that I thought at the beginning—with the network beginning and the work we did, for a time, to try and shut down Rikers—that campaigns against jail expansion could be this massive, watershed, moment for local organizing capacity for abolitionist demands. And in the course of some of this reflection, especially with other people who have participated in campaigns, I now feel like a lot of these jail-expansion campaigns and or campaigns to stop construction are more like entry points, rather than the ultimate goal. Even when the demand is decarceration, the terms on which this decarceration happens, aka "how we reduce and get people out of jail," "how we stop people going in" begin at the level of "how do we get people fed" and "how do we get people housed?" without compromise. Saying "Hey, there's a jail in your community, and you should care about that and you should try to get rid of it, or you should try to stop other ones from happening" is really an entry point into a much more expansive series of considerations about the world and life, because there are so many things that need to happen after that point to make sure that another jail, another form of coercion or soft policing, does not emerge out of the organizing. And I don't think I would have thought that, four years ago.

Lydia: We would love for you to walk us through what's been happening with the Women's Justice Center in Harlem. To begin, can you speak to how the proposal traveled to New York from Texas and what that relationship is there? It seems like an example of why it's important to think about how the makers of carceral expansion are strategizing across geographies as well.

Mon: It's not just that it traveled from Austin to New York, but also both cities were examples of the trend around carceral humanism and mental health jailing, sanism, and the concept of needing differentiated jails for different conditions or populations. It's all stuff that has been going on for hundreds of years but also a common current trend in many cities. It just so happened that there's organizational relationships between the academic institutions in Austin and those that are in New York. The Columbia Justice Center and the Prison and Jail Innovation Lab at the University of Texas–Austin worked on these proposals and were in conversation about this kind of reformist strategy. And that's, I think, how it got to New York. But typically, I think things go *from* New York *out* into the world.

There is a real genealogy now over the last twenty years between the death of Kalief Browder, the commission to close down Rikers, the campaign to shut down Rikers, the death of Layleen Polanco, the borough jails, the Chinatown campaign to stop the jails, and now the women's jail. It's not surprising that it made it from Austin to New York considering that there's been a massive scramble in New York City for the last ten years to figure out how to be at the cutting edge of jailing and incarceration. The correctional leadership here, the mayors, are really preoccupied with making New York this bastion of "progressive punishment." And I think, yeah, that's probably why it made it here.

Judah: Thanks for laying that out. Can you tell us what exactly the proposal is? What are its NYC origins? What has been the organizing around it?

Mon: It's a developing campaign. Sometime in mid-2022, there was an op-ed published in the *New York Times* called "What Would a Feminist Jail Look Like?" and it caused a lot of uproar across the city and the country. The proposal was very unclear. It was never published as an official proposal that the city was moving forward with but rather was put forward by the Columbia Justice Center and the Women's Community Justice Association. This was developing from a campaign to close Rosie's, or the Rose M. Singer jail, on Rikers Island. It was also tied to the plan to close down

Rikers and build four new borough-based jails. Essentially, proponents of the plan argued that instead of having trans people and gender-nonconforming people and cis women in the same jail that was going to be built for cis men, there should be a different center, a "Women's Justice Center" that looked at incarceration from a more holistic perspective. And they did not call it a jail. This was why they said it would be more "feminist," because it would get people who had long sentences, who are essentially waiting to be sent upstate into a more rehabilitative setting where they had psychiatric support, therapists, counselors, and social workers.

There were a lot of reasons people opposed this. People saw it as an attempt to innovate new ways to jail people of marginalized genders and that this was basically a thinly veiled jail expansion and innovation project. The Columbia Justice Center had people who claimed abolition, but for some reason had participated in the designing of this proposal. People were also discussing the idea implied by the proposal that the men who are also incarcerated on Rikers deserve to be inside and in a less rehabilitative setting, that they're all violent and abusive and would inevitably assault someone. People saw this as a carceral and anti-Black way to think about incarceration itself. People also were bringing up the history of things such as the Women's Prison Association, the Women's House of Detention. People like Craig Gilmore and Laura Whitehorn were like, "We have been fighting gendered punishment for twenty years." So there was a lot of context for people getting upset.

But one of the main catalysts for such a large response was the involvement of the Columbia Justice Center, and so many prominent abolitionists have relationships to Columbia and to academia in general. A loose group of people, including me, some people from Survived and Punished and other organizers drafted a public letter and a week of action targeting Vincent Schiraldi, who used to be the DOC

Commissioner and then was staff at the Columbia Justice Center, as well as targeting other people at the Columbia Justice Center. And this really took off; I think it had one thousand signatories. In the organizing of that letter, there were a lot of conversations about the design of a campaign and a coalition. One series of questions that came up included: "What does it say if we mostly have academics and prominent abolitionists sign this letter? Who is it for and to? How much should we condemn some of the people involved? Should we just say 'abolish Rikers'? How much should we acknowledge the borough-based new jail plan? Should we reflect or mention the organizing that's happened around Rikers in the last ten years? Or is that too much information? Who should we even direct this letter to with all of the signatories?" The letter ultimately came out demanding an end to pretrial detention. It was signed by a lot of people and made the rounds. Interestingly, while it made a lot of noise among the people who signed it, like abolitionist organizers and academics, it didn't receive much reporting and wasn't picked up by journalists. It really functioned more as a political education tool and as a way to reach people who had connections, and I think it worked. It was a really different campaign than No New Jails NYC. Everything that we're talking about happened off of major social media platforms and media publications, but rather through relationships and networks and conversations.

At that time, people were mostly taking issue with the concept of a gender-specific jail endorsed by people who were saying they were abolitionists. At that point, Columbia students successfully organized for the Columbia Justice Center to disaffiliate. The center was taken off the site, its logo was taken off the materials and its leadership said that the center never meant to be so closely associated with this and that it was all a big misunderstanding. At that time, the coalition came together more formally with a lot of questions: "What are our demands? It's fine to say we don't want a new jail, but do we want to empty Rosie's? What kind of strategies are we pushing for? How do we make sure that gender-marginalized people who are detained on Rikers for years do not have to choose between going to a different jail or being inside the Queens facility?" We had a lot of conversations around what our commitments would be ultimately, which mainly concerned keeping people of marginalized genders out of Rikers. That was hard, because that's a much bigger project than stopping a proposal.

The coalition also had a lot of conversations around who we should involve. The reason that this focused on Harlem and Columbia was because the building that they were considering was in Harlem, but they could just decide to build it somewhere else or in another old jail. That was also something we talked about a lot—do we need to have Harlem organizations represented in this coalition or not? One of the things that happened that was really significant was that the executive director of the Women's Community Justice Association, who runs the Beyond Rosie's campaign and who came up with the proposal for the women's jail, was open to meeting with us and other folks from the coalition, including members of the National Council on Incarcerated and Formerly Incarcerated Women and Girls, who already had a relationship with WCJA. Of particular significance to this are relationships between formerly incarcerated women who played a huge role in the direction of this campaign, including women who were pushing for the jail and abolitionist women who were against it. There was a lot of sisterhood that reached across conflict. I think this is because of people like Andrea James and Laura Whitehorn, Virginia Douglas and some of the leadership at the Women's Community Justice Association. It was both a blessing and a challenge.

I think the biggest tensions emerged when some of the other people from the coalition said that we didn't really believe in alternatives to incarceration either. We didn't want just some other kind of facility, but rather preferred the building to become housing or something like that. All of us were really excited about something like the Women's Building in San Francisco. But they took issue with the fact that we were saying that courts and judges also don't have a place in an abolitionist vision. And therefore we didn't really want decarceration. That became a tension in the conversation. I think we did a lot of work to try and say, "There's just different visions here for how we get to the thing that we both want." But the whole experience, I think, is a lesson in co-optation. Because without any kind of public acknowledgment that they were willing to jail and any kind of public commitment to abolitionist strategies, they got to benefit from our collaboration without distancing themselves from the original proposal.

Yes, movement conflict isn't great. But we don't owe it to WCJA to work with them on designing an alternative use for this building when that was never the purpose of the coalition. We were set up to stop the construction of a new women's jail in New York, not to design a facility that would be used to house a population. That distinction was blurred. But it's an interesting consideration for strategy because you always hear "organize your opponents." But this whole experience has raised the question of "well, can we really partner if we have fundamentally different understandings as two groups?" Plus, they're a whole organization with staff, and we're a coalition of people who got together six months ago. So that's where that stands right now.

Judah: Was their argument about your disciplined take on not working with criminal justice officials like judges that, in order to achieve decarceration, you have to work through certain channels within the existing system—i.e., judges and courts?

Mon: We weren't even saying that we opposed any project that works through the courts or with judges. We were just saying that, as a coalition, we don't believe in this system at all. We're always going to be opposed to things that use the system in ways that expand the scope of policing and incarceration. They just felt frustrated because they were like, "Well, you're not really leaving a lot of vehicles for decarceration." Around the time I wrote an article about this, where the crux of the argument essentially was that decarceration is not a stand-in for abolition. I think there's a lot of shared goals in terms of getting people out. But they're not essentially the same thing. And they felt antagonized by the idea that we were leaving them with no tools to achieve decarceration.

Lydia: It's helpful to see that there's this genealogy to the jail proposal and the organizing against it, as well as important tensions. Because so much of what we've been tracking across this book with all the different folks who have written chapters or who we've interviewed, is that everyone's fight, even if it seems like it's two years, it's actually five or ten. And many are also navigating similar political tensions.

Mon: The more I organize around prison-industrial-complex abolition, Rikers, and Black power in New York City, the more I recognize that this is now forty years of people trying to shut down Rikers. Since the 1970s there have been different campaigns to shrink Rikers, and to close the penal colony. The most successful period of decarceration was between 2000 and 2010 when the bed capacity went down so dramatically, but simultaneously New York City's carceral capacity only grew post the recession in the 1970s, the crime bill, and 9/11. Even though fewer people were in jail total between the 1990s and the 2010s, the city is now able to criminalize and arrest more people—family policing expanded, data collection and data sharing increased, psychiatric criminalization grew, as did the power of criminal and drug courts—even as the city has experienced massive levels of homelessness and unemployment, particularly among

Black and immigrant New Yorkers. I say this to reemphasize that efforts to shut down old jails, or stop new ones, have to be couched in a larger affirmative project and long-term vision, and these kinds of campaigns—as I said before—are entry points rather than goals in and of themselves. Even if we had successfully stopped the city council from approving the construction of four new jails in NYC in 2019, we would have still had to contend with all the jails on Rikers, the NYPD, the technocratic surveillance, the courts, and more. Even more so now, because COVID-19 and the uprising have demonstrated that the state will nimbly capture radical critique or has already preempted dissent into its vision of a policing-fueled future. Now, in New York City, there's an influx of proposals and programs designed to get people out of jail, but into supervised release or work release or some other form of social control. Some of the lessons coming out of LA, for example, are around how a campaign goes from being, like, "We don't want a jail" to being like, "We have built multimillion-dollar alternatives to incarceration infrastructure." That is becoming such a huge challenge for jail-expansion organizing and is one of the reasons that people in the network are going to have to discuss that, although the original goals of the network were to try and prevent these kinds of co-options and neoliberal devolutions, they're happening all the time, rapidly—and what preemptive strategies do we build with this knowledge?

Conclusion: Fighting the New Geography of Mass Incarceration

Jack Norton, Lydia Pelot-Hobbs, and Judah Schept

The stories of anti-jail campaigns compiled in this book are only a snapshot of the struggles against jails and criminalization happening across the United States. We know that in dozens of other places—from Austin, Texas, to Bloomington, Indiana; from Los Angeles, California, to Bangor, Maine—people have and continue to resist public resources being diverted into locking more people up. Grassroots activists are challenging the narrative that jails can ever be a site of care or a solution to the political economic crises endemic to racial capitalism. In doing so, they are clarifying the multifaceted and everyday state violence of jailing while demanding the creation of a new kind of world: one free from cages, capitalist abandonment, and premature death, one invested in social infrastructure that fosters and extends collective life.

While this might sound utopian, anti-jail organizers are steadily building toward this abolitionist horizon in ways big and small. Through holding teach-ins, knocking on doors, conducting research, showing up at public hearings, organizing protests, drafting policy, and more, activists are disrupting the centrality of criminalization and incarceration to local governance and forging a new common sense of what communities need for their shared safety and well-being. People are building relationships and linking struggles across a range of issues, from addiction to housing to immigration policing to the feminization of poverty. In making these connections, organizers are highlighting the multiple and material harms of the jail while deepening solidarities and developing shared political commitments.

Incarceration is class war, and fights against jail expansion— whether in small towns, major cities, or suburban communities —are a front line of anti-racist class struggle. In other words, jail campaigns, while local, are anything but provincial. Anti-jail organizers and activists are contesting the routinization of carceral regimes, the crises of austerity, the hardening of borders, and the reframing of the jail as the only legitimate site of social provision. Through this organizing, people are illuminating how the jail serves as a node of permanent war at home and abroad. As the stories in this book have detailed, grassroots opposition to jailing is pivotal to making abolitionist geographies.[1]

As the jail is everywhere, then everywhere and anywhere is poised for a jail struggle. Our modest hope is that this book might be a resource for those facing jail proposals in their communities. Toward that end, we draw together what lessons the anti-jail activism outlined in this book can teach us about the contemporary terrain of struggles against local jails and the broader carceral state, as well as the conditions of possibility for abolitionist gains.

Jail Fights Are Fights over Planning and Development

When elected officials and local elites plan to build a new jail or to expand a jail, they are planning for a future in which more and more people will be detained, incarcerated, and criminalized. When they actually build the jail, they are turning

---

1 Ruth Wilson Gilmore, "Abolition Geography and the Problem of

this carceral vision into reality, changing the facts on the ground, and creating the infrastructure for mass detention and criminalization. Jail boosters—local elites, jail consultants, jail architects, county sheriffs—will often talk about rising incarceration as if it simply happens, like the weather, and that it is their job to respond with more investment in police and jails. The reality, however, is that jail incarceration rates result from policy decisions and local priorities. Fights over jail construction are fights over planning and development, and activists fighting against incarceration and criminalization are working to build safer communities and lives worth living.

Incarceration is class warfare, and "tax struggle is the oldest form of class struggle."[2] New or expanded jails are often one of the most significant capital expenses that a county or city will undertake, whether it is $11 billion for borough-based jails in New York City, or $100 million for a new jail in a smaller city, or less than that (or more) for a rural jail. Counties and cities will almost always bond out to pay for jail construction, which is to say they will use public debt to pay for construction, and public money to pay for operating costs. Laws and policies around public debt vary by state, and even by county, and the financing schemes and mechanisms available to jail boosters will vary depending on the locality. Jail boosters may propose to pay for a jail with a regressive sales tax, or with a more progressive county income tax. They may attempt to finance jail construction through a lease-purchase agreement with a public authority, or through a revenue bond backed by a contract with a federal agency. Sometimes, county officials will need to hold a public referendum in order to go into the debt required for carceral expansion. As the activists and scholars in these

---

Innocence," in *Futures of Black Radicalism*, ed. Gaye Theresa Johnson and Alex Lubin (London: Verso Books, 2017).

2 Ruth Wilson Gilmore, "Globaslisation and US Prison Growth: From Military Keynesianism to Post-Keynsian Militarism," *Race and Class* 40 (1999): 182.

chapters have demonstrated, jail fights are struggles over local development, and the financing of jail infrastructure is political. Jail expansion is never inevitable, and anti-jail strategy almost always requires some attention to the details of local budgets and an engagement with local development policy.

Anti-Jail Fights Require Ideological Struggle

Jail fights occur on different terrains of struggle. Often, an over-crowded jail precipitates plans for a new one, whether through appeals to conscience or because of the threat of a lawsuit or consent decree. At other times, the prospect of holding people detained by a state department of corrections or federal agency, as well as the very real lure of revenue, stimulates local leaders to pursue expansion. Certainly, perceived increases in crime—grounded or not in real increases—can generate momentum toward new or expanded jails.

All of the arguments for jail expansion or new jail construction require anti-jail organizers to engage in ideological struggle. That is, in addition to political education around budgets, tax and criminal justice policy, and law, anti-jail organizers work on the level of consciousness, to upend the "common sense" of jails that has been built over five decades of mass incarceration. At numerous points along the way of trying to build a jail, ideology works to try and shore up the kinds of questions, inconsistencies, and weaknesses that would otherwise undermine its credibility.

It follows that anti-jail activists pursue numerous points of intervention:

- Against the claims that overcrowded jails are indicators that a city needs more bed space, we argue that over-crowding evidences the criminalization of poverty and an overreliance on cages. Building new jails to alleviate overcrowding doubles down on a carceral solution to a carceral problem.

- Against appeals for new or expanded jails to accommodate state prisoners or federal detainees to pursue available revenue, we argue that jails are shallow, violent, and unreliable development "solutions." Jails are expensive to build and operate, and the projected per diem payments from a state DOC or ICE are not necessarily guaranteed. Changes in state corrections or federal immigration policies may significantly affect a given jail's population of these prisoners from outside the county. In other words, jails, like prisons, are not the "recession-proof" development strategy their boosters often promise.

- In response to appeals for more jail space because of real or perceived increases in crime, we point to changing police recording or patrol practices, larger changes in political economy (like job losses), or cuts to social services. Indeed, jail itself—its existing operating budget, projected construction costs, to say nothing of what it does to people—makes communities less safe by diverting funds from other places and subjecting people to slow and occasionally immediate violence. Moreover, local reporting may uncritically parrot police framing and talking points, helping to create an often racist sense of threat and risk that jail boosters can then steer into building support for more cages (and more cops). Local newspapers and social media offer crucial places to interrupt and challenge dominant framing of these issues.

- In response to appeals that increased jail space will enable a given community to provide better care to marginalized populations (women, trans and nonbinary people, people with mental health issues, folks dealing with drug addiction, youths, and so on), we keep front and center that any and all incarceration is state violence. Therefore, infrastructures of care need to be developed with a focus on people's self- and collective-determination provided in noncoercive environments. Care cannot be found within a cage but through meaningful investments that reduce people's vulnerabilities and precarities.

Struggles against jails and prisons demonstrate that there isn't an established chronology to the relationship between ideological and material change. It may be that in some places, political education to disrupt the idea that, for example, a big new jail is not the answer to problems of overcrowding, helps to persuade once or would-be supporters of construction away and toward alternatives. In other contexts, people's opposition to new taxes or to an unsightly construction project may make them sympathetic to anti-jail sentiment, and further ideological efforts may help organize them into a campaign. The point is that important ideological work doesn't necessarily prefigure material struggle. It isn't necessarily the case, for example, that we first change hearts and minds and then change policy and practice. The jail is firmly integrated into municipal planning, development, and governance, and therefore our efforts have to target it in those very concrete relationships. In the course of our campaigns—from formal political education workshops to interventions in media to door-knocking efforts to social media posts—we work dialectically to shape conditions on the ground as well as the ways in which our communities understand them.

Anti-Jail Struggles Are Iterative and Long-Haul

Campaigns to close a jail or stop a new one from being built or expanded are not singular events. Because of the confluence of forces aligned around jailing and the various policies and politics that converge to emplace a jail in the landscape, struggles against jails are by definition iterative and long-haul.

Jail proposals that were at one point defeated are routinely resurrected, whether by officials doubling down on carceral humanism when putting a jail expansion tax back on local ballots or by moving the decision from voters to county and city officials. In other instances, grassroots activists have succeeded in convincing local officials to stop a jail plan only to find themselves in the crosshairs of federal judges demanding jail expansion in the name of restoring incarcerated people's constitutional rights. Furthermore, jail plans travel across space and time. For instance, when Austin activists shut down the University of Texas's Prison and Jail Innovation Lab's proposition for a "trauma-informed" women's jail, the proposal was repackaged and proposed as a new "feminist jail" in Harlem, New York. And at other times, such as in Jackson County, Oregon, a seemingly intractable jail plan was shut down through the slow and steady work of community organizing.

Yet naming these obstacles is not to be defeatist. The reality that there isn't a silver bullet is not a drawback but an opportunity for abolitionist organizing. As jailing infrastructures are produced through a series of decisions and systems, there are a host of points of intervention for abolitionist activism. In the words of Xochitl Bervera and Wes Ware, this work can look like "starving the beast," or reducing the number of people locked up in a jail. This can include decriminalizing offenses on the municipal, county, and state levels; eliminating cash bail as a step toward the eradication of pre-trial detention; fights to reduce the size, scope, and power of police; ending contracts between state departments of correction and sheriff's offices; canceling federal contracts with ICE and the US Marshals; and much more. While reducing the number of people caged is pivotal for challenging one of the primary arguments for new jails —overcrowding—it does not promise that officials will stop promoting jails. Hence, anti-jail organizers must be adept at maneuvering the often mundane politics of land-use policy,

THE JAIL IS EVERYWHERE

from canvassing against new jail taxes to learning the county planning procedures to conducting political education about the false promises of jails as economic development or sites of care. These multipronged tactics are likely to be deployed and refined over months and years, shaping and influencing one another as political conditions shift and transform.

At the same time, organizers must be shrewd about how policymakers offer new carceral innovations when jailing has lost favor. As James Kilgore reminds us, reforms like electronic monitoring extend punitive state control. Drug courts can further legitimize the criminalization of drug use. In other words, the long-haul work of jail struggles pushes us to contest not only the physical jail but the carceral logics and practices that devalue the dignity and worth of certain people and places.

Anti-Jail Strategy Requires Study of Geographical and Political Context

Jails are situated at local or regional scales. As these chapters make clear, jail fights are intensely local, and knowledge of city and county politics, histories, and even personalities can make important contributions to anti-jail strategy. Similarly, the contours of local political alignments matter. In some places, jail expansion efforts may be led by law-and-order politicians, both Democrats and Republicans. In other places, carceral humanist Democrats, liberal academics, robust nonprofit organizations, and even formerly incarcerated people might lead the charge for a new jail. Anti-jail activists might have to organize would-be allies out of those political alignments and into their own campaign, or identify potentially strange political bedfellows, like anti-tax or anti-spending Republicans. Likewise, these chapters make clear that both the structure and language of anti-jail efforts will look different in different places. In one community, it may make sense to form a broad coalition, where defeating the jail unites members across what might be considerable political differences. In another, anti-jail efforts will be most forceful in the form of an explicitly abolitionist campaign or organization.

The local politics that shape these decisions matter, and it is critical to understand them. But jail fights are not provincial. Local jail expansion efforts are sometimes responses to and expressions of broader patterns within a given state; jails may also align with national trends. The volume of organizers encountering some degree of "carceral humanism" in this book speaks to the need to understand how shifting populations, practices, or logics at various scales may make an impact on your community. Moreover, with jails condensing multiple arenas of political decision-making and power, organizers must understand the ins and outs of these different political jurisdictions and mechanisms. For instance, as jails are sites of federal detention and in many places state imprisonment, the conditions of struggle may require scaling up political opponents to include organizing against ICE or state legislatures that put such devolution strategies in motion.

As these chapters have made clear, jails condense multiple crises. On its face, a given jail construction proposal may be in response to deteriorating conditions or overcrowding at an existing facility. But as we know, jails have become purported solutions for everything from addiction to mental health, from unemployment to development. As such, fighting them requires principled and committed study of the crises themselves. How might new fronts of the drug war affect a jail expansion effort? How might a new jail be tied to neighborhood "revitalization" efforts? What might a jail proposal in your community have to do with debt, revenue, or infrastructure?

Your jail fight matters. It is at the center of the struggle against mass incarceration. Jails rely on criminalization and incarceration to address crises of development, deindustrialization, public health, and public education. They make those crises worse. To defeat plans for a new or expanded jail in your county of 10,000 people, or in your city of 10 million, is to organize a different future, the one that all of us deserve and that we can build together.

Acknowledgments

The editors have much appreciation for those who have supported this project. First and foremost we are grateful to the contributors to this volume for sharing their rich stories and analysis, and for showing how people are crafting freedom in the here and now. Ruth Wilson Gilmore's research and thinking on carceral and abolitionist geographies deeply shaped this volume, and we are grateful for and honored by her foreword. Craig Gilmore, Naomi Murakawa, and Jessie Kindig's generous engagement and feedback helped to get this project off the ground; Rosie Warren's steady support helped to guide it home. In addition, this book has been influenced by ongoing conversation and political work with comrades, colleagues, and friends: thank you, Byron Asher, Michelle Brown, Orisanmi Burton, Jordan Camp, Brooke Gentile, Bea Halbach-Singh, Christina Heatherton, Micah Herskind, Rachel Herzing, Stephen Jones, Jacob Kang-Brown, Zhandarka Kurti, Carmen Mitchell, Hilary Moore, Camille Rudney, Sylvia Ryerson, Ashley Spalding, Jarrod Shanahan, Monica Smith, David Stein, Hadass Wade, Tyler Wall, and Jess Zhang.

Appendix

The County Jail

I.

The jail is full … Tonight behind those walls
A man turns over, scratches and turns back
Again upon his bunk, while through a crack
Along the cell, to their weird carnivals,
Come beady-eyed gray mice and their foot-falls
Flutter along the floor … Beside a rack
Of rifles in the office, with a pack
Of cards, are deputies. And time crawls.

Earth's jails were full a thousand years ago.
The Bastille fell. Where Torquemada's deep
Abysmal dungeons reeked now flowers may grow.
Too old is this grim habit which men keep,
Too dark this jail so silent with its woe,
Where guards play poker so they will not sleep!

II.

"Rich man, poor man, beggar man, thief;
Doctor, lawyer, merchant, chief!"

The jail is in their lives. Throughout six days
The rich man loves it as he loves his church
On one. The poor man hates it with his head
And heart and fists. The blind, unending search
Of beggars through the perilous, paved maze
Of streets is to escape it—their gray dread.

The thieves that lie in it find it a part
Of living. Like the invalid's fierce pain
It is endured. Oh, two or three obscene
And dreary sentences are not in vain,
The theory is, if one's persistent heart
May hold brief celebration in between!

The doctor takes the pulses in the cells,
Then takes his fee. And with more fees than wits
The lawyers, snarling in their courts, distort
Men's lives. The merchant sells clubs, guns and
writs.
The chief, the county sheriff, vainly swells
With pride; the jail is full by his report.

III.

The jail was built by workers for their friends
Who, sickened by the thought of work in shops,
Might take to jobs annoying to the cops.
Brick-layers built the stairway that descends
To dungeons, built the doorway that portends
Of bugs or floggings. Hunkies, Yankees, Wops,
Whose widows someday will be pushing mops,
May see their own sons here before life ends.

So old among us here this jail has grown
That even now there in the cells, in gray,
May be a man whose father built with stone
The high walls; one whose father hauled the clay
For those dark bricks that close him in; or one
Whose father wired the gongs that mark his day.

Stanley Boone
Liberator 7, no. 9 (September 1924)
marxists.org